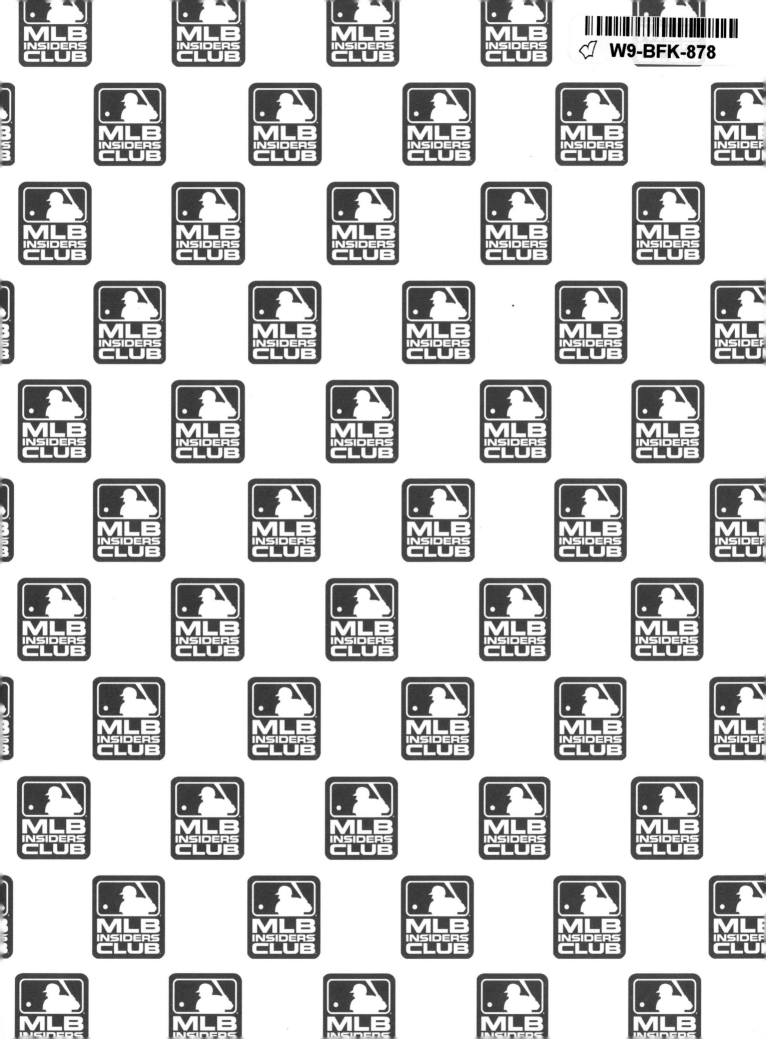

W9-BFK-878

INSIDE
the world series

A behind-the-scenes look at the Fall Classic.

Baseball Insiders Library™

INSIDE
the world series
A behind-the-scenes look at the Fall Classic.

MLB INSIDERS CLUB ®

Baseball Insiders Library™

INSIDE THE WORLD SERIES by Pete Williams
A behind-the-scenes look at the Fall Classic.

Printed in 2009

ABOUT THE AUTHOR
Pete Williams has covered baseball for nearly two decades for numerous media outlets, including USA Today, The New York Times, SportsBusiness Journal *and* Fox Sports. *The author or co-author of nine books, he has covered or attended eight World Series. The Virginia native lives in Safety Harbor, Fla., with his wife and two sons.*

ACKNOWLEDGEMENTS
Major League Baseball would like to thank Pat Kelly and Milo Stewart, Jr., at the National Baseball Hall of Fame and Museum for their invaluable assistance; as well as Eric Enders, Bill Francis, Nathan Hale and Kristin Nieto for their diligent work in helping to prepare this book for publication.

A huge debt of gratitude also goes out to the employees of Major League Baseball and the Clubs for being so generous with their time, and to the entire MLB public relations team for its monumental support along the way. All insights from these individuals were crucial to telling the story behind the World Series.

MAJOR LEAGUE BASEBALL PROPERTIES
Vice President, Publishing
Donald S. Hintze

Editorial Director
Mike McCormick

Publications Art Director
Faith M. Rittenberg

Senior Production Manager
Claire Walsh

Associate Editor
Jon Schwartz

Associate Art Director
Melanie Finnern

Senior Publishing Coordinator
Anamika Chakrabarty

Project Assistant Editors
Chris Greenberg, Jodie Jordan

MAJOR LEAGUE BASEBALL PHOTOS
Director
Rich Pilling

Photo Editor
Jessica Foster

MLB INSIDERS CLUB
Creative Director
Tom Carpenter

Managing Editor
Jen Weaverling

Prepress
Wendy Holdman

1 2 3 4 5 6 7 8 9 10 / 12 11 10 09
Copyright © MLB Insiders Club 2009
ISBN: 978-1-58159-417-1
All rights reserved. No part of this publication may be reproduced, stored in an electronic retrieval system or transmitted in any form or by any means (electronic, photocopying, recording or otherwise) without the prior or written permission of the copyright owner.

MLB Insiders Club
12301 Whitewater Drive
Minnetonka, MN 55343

TABLE OF CONTENTS

INTRODUCTION

WITH A HISTORY SPANNING MORE THAN A CENTURY, THE WORLD SERIES IS ONE OF THE BIGGEST events in sports. The best club from the American League began battling the top team from the National League in the World Series more than a decade before the NBA, NHL or NFL had even played a single game. The passion, both on and off the field, has only increased as the years have passed, raising a humble bat-and-ball game to a national pastime. Often lasting more than a week, the World Series requires behind-the-scenes efforts of hundreds of people to set the stage. And it's thanks to the tireless work of thousands more during the event that the Fall Classic is able to produce memories that are passed on from generation to generation.

Although the players are the ones who are long remembered for their performances in October, the team toiling out of sight plays an equal part in making the Fall Classic a spectacular affair. Major League Baseball's employees, representatives from the participating clubs and folks from myriad professions come together to create the pageantry befitting Cooperstown-worthy performances like Reggie Jackson's three-homer explosion in Game 6 of the 1977 World Series, which cemented for him the nickname "Mr. October," or Bill Mazeroski's dramatic, Series-clinching home run in Game 7 of the 1960 World Series.

Admittedly, other professional sports have their marquee moments. Super Bowl Sunday attracts a massive worldwide audience, as the NFL's championship game has become a virtual national holiday in the United States. But the Super Bowl remains a one-day event, no matter how entertaining.

The Masters Golf Tournament is perhaps the toughest ticket in sports, played at picturesque Augusta National Golf Club, and can even rival a four-game World Series sweep in length. But the early rounds at Augusta don't produce legendary moments equivalent to Don Larsen's perfect game in Game 5 of the 1956 World Series or Kirk Gibson's Game 1 home run in 1988.

The Daytona 500 is the granddaddy of all NASCAR races, attracting more than 165,000 spectators to Daytona Beach, Fla., each February. But since it's just the first race of the stock car season, one of 36 in the top circuit, a win there means little more than a Big League team opening the year 5-0.

The one-of-a-kind drama of the Fall Classic allows a player to become synonymous with baseball's championship round more so than in any other sport. Gibson and Larsen enjoyed lengthy, successful careers, but are best known for their famous World Series moments. The same is true for Mazeroski, whose eight Gold Glove Awards take a back seat to one life-altering trip to the plate. Such Herculean performances are remembered, in part, because of the unforgettable nature of the Series. Each thread of the Classic is meticulously weaved together and tied to baseball's storied history.

"The depth of history and tradition surrounding the World Series gives it a cultural relevance greater than any other sporting event," said Tim Brosnan, Major League Baseball's executive vice president for business.

For many fans, it's doesn't feel like the World Series until they've seen the logo patches sewn onto a player's cap, even a dirty well-worn lid. It's not the World Series without champagne celebrations in the clubhouse, Series logos stenciled on the field, blimps circling overhead, and plenty of bunting — U.S. flag bunting, that is.

From the clubhouse workers tending to the players to the groundskeepers dressing the field, to the singing of the national anthem and the tossing out of the ceremonial first pitch, the pageantry that has become synonymous with October baseball is no accident. The World Series is a well-oiled machine, from the minute-by-minute pregame schedule to the distribution of World Series champion clubhouse gear just moments after the last out of the clinching game.

And although each World Series ends there, ripples from the event continue for days, even months. Not long after the clubhouse celebrations and victory parades, preparations for the following Fall Classic are well underway, continuing a year-long cycle of planning that culminates in the next World Series.

GAME 1: TO THE DRAWING BOARD

Baseball fans used to camp outside of ticket offices overnight if they wanted a seat at the Fall Classic. Before online lotteries and full-time jobs dedicated to ticketing, fans and even Big League clubs had a different experience preparing for the big event. Today, by the time the All-Star break arrives, people behind the scenes have been planning for the Fall Classic for months.

Major League Baseball launches its marketing campaigns during the Midsummer Classic to begin stoking fan interest. And when September rolls around, contending clubs send scouts to keep tabs on potential October opponents. Meanwhile, clubhouse managers make plans to expand their staffs should the postseason come into sight, and umpire supervisors meet and discuss who is worthy of calling which playoff series. For all parties involved, the preparation for baseball's grandest event begins much sooner than fans would think.

CHICAGO FAITHFUL Fans waiting for tickets to go on sale for the 1935 World Series keep warm as they camp outside Wrigley Field for the night.

MARKETING CAMPAIGNS

MAJOR LEAGUE BASEBALL DOESN'T WAIT UNTIL THE END OF THE REGULAR SEASON TO BEGIN promoting the World Series. These days, the marketing campaign kicks off during the All-Star break, which is appropriate considering the event now determines home-field advantage for the Fall Classic.

"We're using our biggest platform, the All-Star Game, to tell people to stay tuned and be a part of these great emerging races," said Jacqueline Parkes, MLB's chief marketing officer and senior vice president for advertising and marketing.

One of MLB's most recent campaigns, "There's Only One October," began in 2006 and has featured Hall of Famer and former Dodgers Manager Tommy Lasorda, as well as comedian Dane Cook.

In 2008, the marketing campaign featured numerous celebrities, all avid baseball fans, as well as MLB players, in a series of ads in which they were seen at computers crafting blog entries in their own voices about the excitement of October baseball. Images of the celebrities were interspersed with historic postseason moments while the blogs were narrated.

The celebrities included *American Idol* judge Randy Jackson; comedian Frank Caliendo; and comedian Jeff Foxworthy, a longtime Atlanta Braves fan and host of *Are You Smarter Than a Fifth Grader?* The ads ran frequently on the networks that broadcast MLB's postseason.

To incorporate its fan base throughout the 2008 season, MLB surveyed more than 20,000 fans that had registered on MLB.com to be part of "MLB Fans at Bat." In August, more than 80 percent of fans surveyed identified the unlikely turnaround of the Tampa Bay Rays as the top story in baseball. Therefore, the Rays were incorporated into a second element of postseason marketing to make fans more aware of the emerging storylines as the season progressed.

"We're always trying to understand the pulse of the fans, and through our research we're able to leverage that information and put it into the creative side of what we do," Parkes said.

ON THE SET The 2008 postseason marketing campaign featured some of baseball's biggest stars. Above: Torii Hunter (left) and Mark Teixeira. Opposite: Jermaine Dye (left) and A.J. Pierzynski.

HOMETOWN CHAMPS The Cardinals' Albert Pujols (5) and Scott Rolen celebrate their 2006 world championship at home — the first team to clinch in front of their own fans since the '02 Angels.

NO PLACE LIKE HOME

It wasn't too long ago that the schedule for the World Series was set years in advance, with the American League and National League alternating home-field advantage annually as hosts for Games 1, 2, 6 and 7.

But when the 2002 All-Star Game ended in a tie, Commissioner Bud Selig upped the ante of the Midsummer Classic and awarded home-field advantage in the World Series to the winner of the All-Star Game. That seemed like quite an incentive at the time, since the team with home-field advantage had won 15 of 17 World Series from 1985 through 2002, including the eight previous Game 7s.

Although the All-Star Game has certainly been a more spirited affair since Selig's decision, the results have favored the AL, as the Junior Circuit has for the most part dominated the Senior Circuit. Because it takes the full seven games for home-field advantage to truly matter in the World Series, the edge has not been a significant factor since Hank Blalock of the Rangers first clinched it for the AL with a game-winning home run in the 2003 All-Star Game.

That year, the Yankees held home-field advantage but still lost the World Series to the Florida Marlins, who clinched the championship in Game 6 at Yankee Stadium. The Boston Red Sox and Chicago White Sox swept the Series in four games in '04 and '05, respectively. Although the Detroit Tigers held the home-field edge in '06, the St. Louis Cardinals took the title in five games. The Red Sox swept again in 2007, this time taking down the Colorado Rockies. And the Rays couldn't capitalize on the AL's 2008 All-Star Game win during that year's Fall Classic against the Phillies.

Still, the prospect of home-field advantage remains an incentive for All-Star Game participants, no matter how unlikely a World Series berth might seem at the time. In 2008, the Tampa Bay Rays entered the break with a 55-39 record, just a half-game behind the Red Sox in the American League East division. Although the Rays had never won more than 70 games in any of their previous 10 seasons, they harbored realistic hopes of a postseason berth when their club-record three All-Star representatives arrived in New York.

And they certainly helped the cause. Third baseman Evan Longoria tied the All-Star Game with a double in the eighth inning, catcher Dioner Navarro reached base twice, and left-hander Scott Kazmir worked a scoreless 15th to get the win.

"Longoria, Navi and I talked about it when we were there," Kazmir said before the World Series. "We knew this game that we were playing really meant something to us because in the long run it would really give us an advantage, hopefully, for the World Series. You couldn't ask for anything more, especially the way we played here. So in the back of our heads, we knew how much this game meant to us as a team, as an organization."

Alas, the Rays' All-Star efforts and subsequent Fall Classic home-field advantage mattered little as the Phillies clinched their first World Series crown in 28 years, winning Game 5 in Philadelphia. Phillies closer Brad Lidge, who was tagged with the loss in the All-Star Game after allowing the winning run in the 15th inning, was on the mound to record the final out of the Series.

1987 WORLD SERIES — ST. LOUIS CARDINALS vs. MINNESOTA TWINS

It was more than a decade before the American and National Leagues started battling for World Series home-field advantage in the All-Star Game, but home games were certainly important during the 1987 Fall Classic. That year, the St. Louis Cardinals and the Minnesota Twins participated in the first ever World Series in which each and every game was won by the home team. It was also the first World Series to be played indoors, starting at Minnesota's domed stadium, the Metrodome. The Twins started things off with two wins there, and ultimately took the Series in seven games.

Game 1 – Metrodome (Minnesota)	Game 2 – Metrodome (Minnesota)	Game 3 – Busch Stadium (St. Louis)	Game 4 – Busch Stadium (St. Louis)
Cardinals: 1	Cardinals: 4	Twins: 1	Twins: 2
Twins: 10	Twins: 8	Cardinals: 3	Cardinals: 7

Game 5 – Busch Stadium (St. Louis)	Game 6 – Metrodome (Minnesota)	Game 7 – Metrodome (Minnesota)
Twins: 2	Cardinals: 5	Cardinals: 2
Cardinals: 4	Twins: 11	Twins: 4

HOUSE PARTY The Philadelphia
Phillies celebrate after becoming
2008 world champions at Citizens
Bank Park in Philadelphia.

SCOUTING

Ask team officials about the World Series in mid-September, and they'll stress that they're not looking beyond the next game, and certainly not all the way to the postseason.

But in reality, preparations are well underway for a possible World Series appearance. The middle of September is when contending clubs assign scouts to the teams they may face in the Division Series, League Championship Series and even the Fall Classic.

Unlike the mid-summer months of July and August, when scouts often watch the one or two players for whom their teams are considering acquiring via trade, during the later portion of the year scouts shift focus on determining tendencies of potential postseason opponents and how they might play out against their own roster. They pass on information like which pitches hurlers favor in certain situations, or other strengths and weaknesses.

Phillies director of professional scouting Chuck LaMar, the original general manager of the then-Devil Rays through the 2005 season, found himself in the unusual position of assigning scouts to follow the Rays in 2008.

Conveniently for Philadelphia, LaMar had actually drafted, developed or traded for several of the Rays. When the Phillies defeated Tampa Bay in just five games, some credit was given to that scouting team. LaMar says his job has changed little since 1991, when he was director of scouting and player development for the Atlanta Braves.

"The only thing that has changed after all these years is the access to statistical data," he said. "The game has become so much more computerized. But the basic premise of scouts sitting behind home plate and trying to gather tendencies has not changed at all."

The middle of September is when contending clubs assign scouts to the teams they may face in the Division Series, League Championship Series and even the Fall Classic.

WATCH CAREFULLY Tom Yawkey (left) and Joe Cronin (center) scout for the Red Sox at a 1946 game between the Cardinals and Dodgers that would decide the National League champion.

CLUBHOUSE MANAGERS

MOST MAJOR LEAGUE CLUBHOUSE MANAGERS SPEND October winding down their regular-season duties. This involves boxing and shipping personal belongings to players, and thoroughly cleaning an area that has seen heavy use by dozens of grown men for six months.

For the two clubhouse managers whose teams reach the World Series however, such duties are postponed until November while they continue to deal with the usual in-season tasks, this time with hundreds of extra media members in the house.

During the season, clubhouse managers and their assistants provide players with everything they need to play, from clean uniforms and cleats to pre- and post-game meals. The assistants will also run all kinds of personal errands for the ballplayers, the tips for which can often be well worth it.

Those requests are fewer during the World Series as players focus more on the game itself and on dealing with an avalanche of media attention. Even though the clubhouse is closed before the game during the playoffs and World Series, there are exceptions. Television producers and on-air talent have pregame clubhouse access and managers can allow the team's regular beat writers into the office for pregame chats if desired.

Tampa Bay's equipment and clubhouse manager never had to worry about such tasks until the 2008 season, when the Rays went on an unlikely World Series run.

"The post-game crush more than makes up for it," said Chris Westmoreland, the Rays' clubhouse manager. "But it's a nice problem to have. I hope we have it every year."

The workload gets heavier for those staffing the clubhouse when rosters expand to 40 players on Sept. 1, and it doesn't let up in October. Although teams must name a 25-man roster for each postseason series, they typically continue to dress injured players and those who didn't quite make the 25-man cut. Some teams will even dress two or three September call-ups to give them a taste of the World Series, even if they're not on the roster.

To absorb the extra responsibility, Westmoreland, like other clubhouse managers, added two extra assistants to his five-man staff for the 2008 post-season. Most modern clubhouses are spacious, but even the largest rooms can feel cramped when more than 100 media members arrive for post-game interviews. Clubhouse managers need more help — and more space. They often move furniture from the locker room. Most teams have private areas that are off-limits to the media anyway, so this generates few protests.

Except for the additional post-game media horde and the stray World Series logo or patch, the clubhouse atmosphere is actually quite similar to that of the regular season. That's by design, given the almost obsessive routines that athletes tend to follow.

"I noticed a lot of players didn't change their schedules or routines," Westmoreland said. "They're so focused on the Series and that particular game, they don't have time to think about anything else."

A WORLD SERIES DAY IN THE LIFE OF A CLUBHOUSE MANAGER

Jim Schmakel has been in Detroit's clubhouse for two of the club's Fall Classic appearances, keeping things in order in 1984 and 2006.

10–11:30 a.m.: Arrive at the ballpark; set up lunch; make sure clean uniforms and other laundry has been placed in player lockers.

12–4 p.m.: Distribute packages and mail to player lockers (there is usually more during the Series, as suppliers send new bats, shoes, etc.); have an attendant rub baseballs for the umpires — at least 12 dozen for a World Series game; maybe go to the stadium lobby to meet a player's family members and escort them in; check the dugout to make sure all the equipment is in position; fulfill equipment, ticket and parking lot requests and secure hotel rooms for players' families and friends.

5:15 p.m.: Make sure players are on the field for batting practice and that they have everything they need. While the team is hitting (40 to 50 minutes), set up more food.

6:50 p.m.: Make sure all players are on the field for throwing, stretching and jogging and, because it's the Fall Classic, for player introductions.

8:30–9 p.m.: Sit in the dugout to watch the first inning.

9–10:30 p.m.: Clean up the clubhouse kitchen and set up post-game food; maybe visit family in the stands for half an inning; watch the game on clubhouse TVs.

10:30 p.m.–12:30 a.m.: As soon as the game ends, be ready to serve hot food to the players; bring food to the umpires; as the clubhouse clears out, oversee attendants who do laundry, polish shoes, vacuum the carpet, take out the garbage and otherwise prepare for the next day.

1 a.m.: Go home.

WAITING GAME. Clubhouse managers and staff make sure that locker rooms and team dugouts are stocked for games.

UMPIRES

Baseball's seven umpire supervisors meet in mid-September and compile a list of umps to work each postseason series, a group selected based on regular-season performance.

HALL OF FAME UMPIRE BILL KLEM WORKED 108 WORLD SERIES games over the course of 18 Fall Classics, including five straight Series from 1911 to 1915. Those are three records that will stand forever.

Klem's marks are safe because today's umpires operate under the collective bargaining agreement in place between MLB and the World Umpires Association, which mandates that umpires cannot work the World Series in back-to-back years.

That's not to suggest that the most qualified umpires are left out of the six-man staff each season. The World Series crew is selected from the pool of 24 umpires who work the Division Series. The 12 chosen for the League Championship Series are not eligible to work the World Series that year.

"The idea is to keep everyone fresh while at the same time not having too long of a layoff," said Jim McKean, a former umpire and now an umpire supervisor. "There used to be a time when you'd only work the World Series after having nearly a month off."

More than half of Major League Baseball's 68 umpires work at least one playoff series each year. Baseball's seven umpire supervisors, six of whom are former Big League umpires, meet in mid-September and compile a list of umps to work each postseason series, a group selected based on regular-season performance.

Those lists are then approved by Vice President of Umpiring Mike Port, MLB Executive Vice President of Baseball Operations Jimmie Lee Solomon and ultimately by Commissioner Bud Selig.

The whole process is slightly easier than it was before 2000, when umpires were merged into one working unit. Umpires were previously assigned to either the American or National League, and it could be complicated to select three umps from each league to make up the six-member World Series crew.

The group is typically a blend of experienced and younger umpires. Tim Welke, a crew chief since 2000, led the team for the 2008 World Series, his fourth. Tim Tschida, who also serves as a crew chief during the regular season, made his third World Series appearance in 2008, as did Jeff Kellogg. Tom Hallion, Kerwin Danley and Fieldin Culbreth each made their World Series debuts.

Umpires receive two pools of money from the postseason. One is shared by all umpires, regardless of who worked, and the other by those who did work. But being chosen in itself is the real honor.

"It's the biggest stage in our profession," said McKean, who worked four World Series during his career. "You have the best teams and the best umpires."

THE BEST OF THE BEST Home-plate umpire Tom Hallion makes a call during a Fall Classic game in 2008 at Citizens Bank Park in Philadelphia. It was his first appearance in a World Series. Two other umpires, Kerwin Danley and Fieldin Culbreth, also made their Fall Classic debuts in '08.

LAST CALL
Umpires can bear the brunt of player frustration or witness pure elation — such as from Kent Hrbek of the 1987 world champion Minnesota Twins — during the World Series.

THE FATHER OF UMPIRES
Bill Klem called Major League games
from 1905 to 1941 — including 18
World Series — and is said to have been
the first to use hand signals as well as
the modern, smaller chest protector.

TRAVELING SECRETARIES

DURING THE REGULAR SEASON, A TEAM'S TRAVELING SECRETARY is responsible for chartering airplanes, booking hotel rooms and arranging ground transportation for a traveling party of roughly 55 to 60 people, a number that includes players, coaches, trainers, broadcasters and support staff.

It's a demanding job, one in which any glitch can mean a delay for road-weary athletes who expect stress-free, first-class travel. Thankfully, much regular-season planning can be done up to a year in advance, since the tentative MLB schedule is usually released to team officials shortly after the previous season's All-Star break.

But the World Series, along with the rest of the postseason, presents a greater challenge. For one, it's not uncommon for a team's entire front office staff to hit the road. Players and coaches will also bring their families. As many as 200 hotel rooms can be required for each club, along with a larger aircraft and additional buses to transport everyone from the hotel to the ballpark.

Advanced planning is necessary to secure such a large block of rooms. Once a team emerges as a legitimate playoff contender, usually by the All-Star break, traveling secretaries will begin making hotel reservations in every city where it could play in October. Reservations are canceled as teams are eliminated from contention.

In a sport filled with notoriously superstitious people who try not to look beyond the next day's game, postseason planning is done quietly by the traveling secretary and his or her staff, especially if that team is not accustomed to competing in the playoffs.

"I made sure I never uttered the 'P-word,'" said Jeff Ziegler, the director of team travel for the Tampa Bay Rays.

Planning travel is a substantially easier task for the Division Series and the League Championship Series, since teams visit those cities during the regular season and traveling secretaries know where to stay. Plus, traveling parties for the first two rounds of the playoffs are usually smaller than those for the World Series. The Fall Classic requires a little more work, since a traveling secretary needs a larger block of hotel rooms, sometimes in cities where he or she is unaccustomed to working.

Although teams currently fly exclusively on charter aircraft throughout the season, there are also occasional changes made to flight arrangements during the Fall Classic. A 737-800 is large enough to handle a team's entire traveling party and equipment during the regular season, but during the World Series a larger plane, such as a 767 series, is enlisted. Depending on the seat configuration, a 767 can carry between 181 and 375 people.

Once everyone has arrived safely at either site of the World Series, the traveling secretary is responsible for the distribution of game tickets. Each player is permitted to purchase up to six for each postseason game, but some will enlist the traveling secretary to help him come up with more. Ticket distribution is a routine procedure during the regular season, but becomes an unenviable task during the postseason.

Traveling secretaries are detail-oriented by nature, but it's tough to prepare for everything. That's what Ziegler discovered in 2008, when a rainstorm in Philadelphia caused Game 5 of the World Series to be suspended indefinitely during the sixth inning. With the Rays already checked out of their Philadelphia hotel rooms in anticipation of returning to Florida, Ziegler had to scramble for lodging late in the game.

Since much of the Rays' front office staff had returned to St. Petersburg after Game 4, he needed a relatively modest 92 rooms, but that was far more than any Philadelphia-area hotel could handle on such short notice. After a flurry of calls, Ziegler was able to secure rooms in Wilmington, Del., at the historic Hotel du Pont, which has hosted the last nine presidents.

"It's one of the nicest hotels we stayed in all year," Rays Manager Joe Maddon later said.

Once Ziegler landed all of the rooms, he then had to retrieve the hundreds of pieces of luggage that were already sitting on the team's Delta charter at the airport. He promptly contacted the trucking company that transported the team's possessions, and the company picked up the bags and took them to the Hotel du Pont, which is located about 40 minutes by car from Citizens Bank Park.

By the time the Rays arrived at the hotel, their luggage was there and the room keys were ready, a smooth ending to one of the bigger travel predicaments in World Series history.

In a sport filled with notoriously superstitious people who try not to look beyond the next day's game, postseason planning is done quietly by the traveling secretary and his or her staff, especially if that team is not accustomed to competing in the playoffs.

SEND OFF New York City Mayor John V. Lindsay (right) with Mets Manager Gil Hodges at LaGuardia Airport, where the Mets prepare to board a plane to Baltimore before the 1969 World Series.

TICKETING

USUALLY WORLD SERIES TICKETS ARE VERY DIFFICULT TO OBTAIN. AND THE TASK OF regulating who gets them is even more so. But sometimes, more fans than usual get their chance to purchase tickets. That's because season-ticket holders have the right to purchase seats for the Fall Classic. If a team only has a modest base of season-ticket holders, their fans are in luck. But in towns like Boston, New York and St. Louis, that base accounts for much of the ballpark.

Another big chunk of tickets, approximately a few thousand for each game, is earmarked for Major League Baseball to use for sponsors and league officials. Television rights holders — who have included NBC, Fox, ESPN and TBS — also receive an allotment, as well as individual teams and the Major League Baseball Players Association.

Players on the two participating teams can purchase up to six tickets each for both home and away games during the Series. All umpires, not just the six working the event, are given the opportunity to buy four per game. But unlike the NFL, where every player in the league can buy two tickets to the Super Bowl, players on non-participating Major League teams are not given special access to purchase tickets.

But since the task of determining who gets to purchase which tickets can be so complicated and challenging, Rob Capilli, Major League Baseball's senior manager of special events, is assigned full-time to ticketing for baseball's jewel events: the World Series and the rest of the playoffs, the All-Star Game and the World Baseball Classic, not to mention many, many regular-season games.

Capilli's group contacts all contending teams shortly after the conclusion of the All-Star break to help them formulate their ticketing plans for the World Series. Because of the expanded playoffs that have been in place since 1995, that's usually about 18 teams — a group that gets whittled down to about a dozen with two weeks left in the regular season.

Each contending team must submit a plan to Capilli detailing the allotment of tickets, as well as which seats will be available, since some sections are converted into an auxiliary press box for the playoffs, which becomes even bigger for the World Series.

"The days of the 70,000-seat stadiums are gone, so the teams really have to detail their plan," Capilli said.

For Division Series and League Championship Series games, MLB provides all teams with a range of ticket prices. The place where each team falls on that scale usually depends on the size of the market and the costs of the regular-season tickets.

Major League Baseball, however, sets the prices for World Series games. A trend began in 2005 where tickets were priced between $90 and $250 per seat per game, with tickets in premium seating areas priced higher.

By the time teams clinch berths in the World Series, clubs have long determined which seats will be available to the general public. Clubs aim to conduct the public sale shortly after securing a place in the Fall Classic to give fans as much time as possible to travel to the event. Even then there isn't much time, especially if a League Championship Series extends to seven games.

The advent of online ticket selling means that fans are no longer forced to camp out overnight or even for several days waiting for tickets to be made available. In recent years, teams have implemented online lotteries, in which fans enter their e-mail addresses on team websites to become eligible to purchase tickets. Winners can log on at appointed times, enter a password and then purchase a designated number of tickets, usually two to four per game.

Tickets that are purchased online can be printed from a home computer and feature barcodes that are scanned at the ballpark gate. The tickets sent to season-ticket holders and issued by MLB look much more traditional. They are produced from a template that's provided by Capilli's office and printed by the host teams with the help of two printing companies which are used by teams throughout baseball.

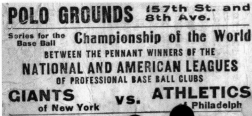

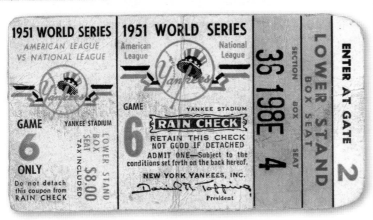

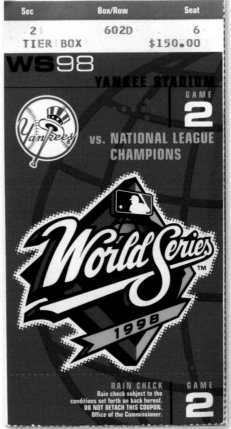

TIMES ARE CHANGING Major
League Baseball works with teams to
plan playoff ticket sales, and fans can
now buy tickets in online lotteries.

PROTECT AND SERVE
New York City police regulate entry
to Yankee Stadium before Game 5
of the 2001 World Series.

SECURITY

WITH PRESIDENT GEORGE W. BUSH THROWING THE FIRST PITCH PRIOR to Game 3 of the 2001 World Series at Yankee Stadium, fans passed through additional security to enter the ballpark. Just weeks after the 9/11 terrorist attacks, nobody complained about the heightened security and delays.

"You went through that security and realized that you were probably in the safest place on Earth at that moment," said Joe Buck, who broadcast the Series for Fox.

MLB tries to provide that high standard of security at every World Series game. When it comes to security for the Fall Classic, it's not just about bag searches, press credentials and security checkpoints. It's about providing a pleasant, family-friendly atmosphere.

"It's our number one goal to ensure the safety and the integrity of the game for our players, their families and our fans," said Earnell Lucas, MLB's vice president of security and facility management.

The World Series presents additional security challenges, though. With so many fans on hand in the host cities, it's even more difficult for players to maneuver between the ballpark and their hotels. There are also many more VIPs and out-of-town fans at each ballpark who are more likely to accidentally stumble into off-limits areas, forcing MLB to upgrade security.

Additionally, each club employs an active law enforcement officer who works part-time for the team, known as a "resident security agent." During the season, the "RSA" handles security issues ranging from game-day staffing to addressing personal threats players might receive.

The RSA also helps further build the relationship between the team and local law enforcement, which becomes especially important during the World Series. Because of the round-the-clock nature of the Fall Classic, RSAs temporarily assume full-time positions with the teams.

"The local agencies have come to know that it's good to have someone working with them," said Lucas, a former RSA for the Milwaukee Brewers. "They have a direct conduit with Major League Baseball and we're better able to share expectations and work together."

RSAs from non-participating clubs help out during the World Series, as well. They escort National Anthem singers and VIPs, and also monitor team hotels for suspicious activities. They assist the umpires and players' families, provide clubhouse support and help with the commissioner's security detail.

During the Series, Lucas begins each morning with a staff meeting, at which topics include transporting players to and from hotels, VIP concerns, and any issues that might impact families of players on the visiting team.

Once a potential clinching game arises, there are more meetings to discuss placement of security personnel in and around the stadium.

At the ballpark, Lucas confers with local law enforcement to make sure everyone is on the same page. During the game, his staff monitors the families of players and umpires to make sure they're not being bothered. The staff monitors alcohol sales and makes sure all media is positioned properly.

"It's a long day and it doesn't conclude until well after the players have left," Lucas said. "I never have a seat and I don't see much of the game. Our job is to make sure everyone else gets to enjoy it."

GAME 2: THE FINISHING TOUCHES

As soon as fans push through the turnstiles or tune in on television, they realize that the World Series is like no other sporting event. The precision with which the outfield grass is manicured and the World Series logo is painted onto the field immediately make clear that the Fall Classic treats both fans and players alike to a near flawless atmosphere.

Clubhouse managers and seamstresses toil far from the spotlight to make certain that everything looks terrific while MLB's designers craft logos for the Fall Classic just as painstakingly as general managers construct rosters. Editors weave together a season's worth of story lines and more than a century's worth of history to produce the official *World Series Program* with the same attention to detail used to produce commemorative shirts and hats. When it comes to the Fall Classic, even the smallest touches are treated with the utmost care.

GROUND CONTROL The Detroit Tigers grounds crew prepares Navin Field for the 1935 World Series.

WORLD SERIES LOGO

THE WORLD SERIES LOGO APPEARS EVERYWHERE DURING THE FALL CLASSIC. IT'S SEWN ONTO uniform sleeves, pressed onto hats, stenciled onto fields and emblazoned onto countless souvenirs, clothing items and printed materials.

With such a high degree of visibility, MLB puts just as much effort and consideration into the design of each year's World Series logo as it puts into the redesign of club logos and uniforms. In both instances, the task falls to Anne Occi, MLB's vice president of design services, and her staff.

The World Series logo must be created about a year in advance and made available by Dec. 1, as much World Series merchandise is produced overseas, and some media outlets like to have the logo for season preview magazines and newspaper special sections. Such a schedule can make it difficult to create an icon that will still look timely by the time the first pitch of the Fall Classic is thrown.

That's why Occi subscribes to several trend-forecasting services that have an uncanny ability to predict upcoming design trends, even a year in advance.

"We'll be able to know what colors will be in style and whether the design should be progressive, retro or conservative," Occi said.

By following trend forecasting, the World Series logo attempts to match the styles of clothing that will be produced for the event. While basic T-shirts vary little, other sportswear evolves, matching better with certain logo styles.

"Certain color waves might be out of style for a particular demographic in menswear or womenswear," Occi said. "With the forecasting, we know we'll be dead-on with what our licensees will be using and can apply our graphic to."

Even the typeset of "World Series" is carefully considered to match the trend forecasting. In 2008, a typeset called ITC Century Handtooled was used, though with some in-house tweaking, it essentially became a hand-drawn font.

The World Series logo was generic until 1978, when a more intricate design was used for the 75th Fall Classic. The logo stayed the same from 1980 to '86, with just the year updated. The pattern of using a nearly identical logo for several years continued from 1987–91, 1992–97 and 1998–99.

From 2001 through 2007, the World Series logo evolved into a modern, progressive, almost space-age look that focused on the international element of "world," much like the logo for the World Baseball Classic.

The logo included the words "Fall Classic" in smaller print on a red banner below "World Series" for the first time in 2008. The design, created by MLB designer Erin Reynolds, also featured a pair of leaves in red and gold representing the AL and NL, and had a traditional look with a heavy dose of green, as the forecast dictated. A secondary logo omitted the red Fall Classic banner.

As usual, the MLB logo of a silhouetted batter was a prominent part of the design, although the color scheme was changed from mostly blue and white with red accents to mostly red and white with green accents. It's part of a recent trend in which MLB has tweaked the color scheme for the World Series and All-Star Game.

After sticking with similar World Series logos for the last two decades of the 20th century, MLB's design team now begins each year with a blank slate, building upon design trends to create a logo that's both timely and classic.

From 2001 through 2007, the World Series logo evolved into a modern, progressive, almost space-age look that focused on the international element of "world," much like the logo for the World Baseball Classic.

UNIFORMS

TEAMS ISSUE NEW UNIFORMS FOR THE WORLD SERIES SO THAT players aren't wearing beat up clothing for baseball's showcase event. Official World Series patches are sewn onto two sets each of both home and away jerseys. Players, managers and coaches usually get to keep one set of each.

Officials from the New Era Cap Co., the official headwear provider of MLB since 1993, affix the World Series emblem to two hats for each player, manager and coach with a heavy-duty steam press machine at the site of the World Series.

Before Major League Baseball applied an authentication system, placing holograms on World Series jerseys and logging each item into a database, the presence of these patches helped authenticate jerseys when they reached the collectibles market.

Throughout the regular season, teams usually enlist the help of a seamster, who will visit the clubhouses on an almost-daily basis to repair uniforms and create jerseys for newly acquired players. This involves sewing on numbers and nameplates. Once a team reaches the World Series, there's suddenly a huge sewing workload. Often, teams employ not just their regular seamstress, but also might bring on additional assistance.

Given the late October schedule of the World Series, additional cold-weather clothing is often needed. Cold-weather caps, which featured built-in earflaps that folded down, much like the hunting headwear worn by cartoon character Elmer Fudd, debuted — and were greatly appreciated — during the 2008 Fall Classic. New Era first issued them during Spring Training before the 2008 season, but they were not worn on the field until Game 5 of the World Series, when rain and cold forced the game to be suspended in the sixth inning for nearly 48 hours. By the time the game was stopped, nearly everyone in uniform had opted for the Elmer Fudd look.

In the Midwest, this style is known as a "Stormy Kromer," named for a former semi-pro baseball player named George "Stormy" Kromer, who worked as a locomotive engineer. In 1903, Kromer asked his wife, Ida, to modify one of his baseball hats for protection against the brutal wintertime winds. Railroad workers and police officers have worn the all-wool creation for years.

> *World Series patches are sewn onto two sets of both home and away jerseys. Players, managers and coaches usually get to keep one set of each.*

ON-FIELD LOGO STENCILING

AS SOON AS A TEAM CLINCHES ITS SPOT IN THE WORLD SERIES, it's a safe bet that newspapers will print a photograph of stadium groundskeepers stenciling the World Series logo onto the field.

Perhaps nothing better signifies that the Fall Classic is on its way. Although the World Series logo is an intricate design featuring up to six colors, the process of stenciling the logo onto the field is a simple one.

World Class Surfaces of Leland, Miss., has provided teams with stenciling kits for the World Series, Super Bowl and other athletic events for years. Groundskeepers receive one stencil for each color and use water-based spray paints to fill in the stencils. The process takes about an hour per logo.

The paint is durable enough for the logos to hold up during precipitation, but has the ability to come off easily when soaked intentionally, allowing for a seamless transition between different rounds of the playoffs.

Of course, the time constraints are sometimes the cause of embarrassing problems. Because teams often want the logos on the field for workout days, a seven-game LCS can force teams to act prematurely. Newspapers in New York had a field day running shots of the 2003 World Series logo behind home plate at Fenway Park after the Yankees won Game 7 of that year's ALCS in dramatic fashion.

CRAFTY WORK Clubs recruit a group of seamsters to embroider World Series patches onto home and away uniforms.

MAN AT WORK Bob Hood paints the 1984 World Series
logo onto the grass at Jack Murphy Stadium in San Diego.

PAINTING THE JAKE Groundskeepers detail
the 1995 World Series logo at Jacobs Field.

HOUSEKEEPING The grounds crew at Veterans Stadium in Philadelphia prepares the infield for play prior to Game 3 of the 1993 World Series.

GROUNDSKEEPERS

FOR THE GROUNDSKEEPERS WHO MAINTAIN MAJOR LEAGUE ballfields, the World Series presents a number of challenges. Among them are late-season weather as well as the hordes of journalists, MLB officials and VIPs who trample the grass during batting practice just a few hours before the surface must be perfect for play and look flawless for a worldwide television audience.

David Mellor, the director of groundskeeping for the Boston Red Sox, is well known around the Big Leagues for the elaborate patterns he and his crew create in the Fenway Park grass, ranging from checkerboards, to the Red Sox logo, to the uniform numbers of Sox stars like Ted Williams, to ribbons in support of awareness for breast cancer and prostate cancer research. Still, the top priority is always the safety and play quality of the field.

"That's always our first concern," said Mellor, whose talents were on display during the 2004 and 2007 World Series. "You never want to harm the grass or affect playability. We rotate patterns so we don't get grains in the grass."

As is standard during the regular season, the grass is cut every day during the World Series when the team is at home so the field plays consistently. A light coating of sand is applied periodically to encourage growth. Such diligent maintenance helps the grass retain its lush green color.

One way groundskeepers protect the field is by placing a geotextile covering over foul territory during batting practice. That can protect the grass for the World Series, although even then the damage often necessitates replacing the turf during the offseason.

A Big League groundskeeper must be able to hide most turf blemishes, which is actually how Mellor developed his patterning system. While working on the Milwaukee Brewers grounds crew in 1993, he had to get the County Stadium turf back in shape after the outfield was ravaged during a Paul McCartney concert.

The process of creating patterns in grass had been around for years but had not been used much in sports. The first lawn mower was made in the 1830s in England, and the striped look on lawns was very popular in Victorian times. Although many people assume that patterns are cut into the grass, they're actually created by using large rollers weighing up to 75 pounds. These rollers are either hand-pushed or affixed to riding mowers to flatten grass.

Since grass blades that are bent away from your vantage point catch more light, they appear lighter in color. Those bent toward your vantage point catch less and appear darker in color. By bending grass in opposite directions, a pattern can be created.

After the McCartney concert, Mellor and his colleagues camouflaged the outfield as best as they could with a checkerboard pattern, and diverted attention with an elaborate design on the infield turf.

When baseball resumed, broadcasters didn't mention damage from the concert, only the pattern in the grass. Soon Mellor was getting calls from viewers everywhere wondering how they could create such patterns in their own lawns. Patterning soon became common at professional sports venues, and in 2001 Mellor published a how-to book about creating patterns for sports fields or residences.

These days, a complete pattern in the grass for the World Series is expected. A pattern was even painted in center field on the Tampa Bay Rays' artificial turf in 2008.

"You have one opportunity to make a first impression, especially during the World Series," Mellor said. "You try and achieve safety and playability first, but there's no doubt we all take a lot of pride in our patterns."

A CUT ABOVE

Red Sox director of grounds David Mellor explained in his book, *Picture Perfect*, how to create three of his top patterns:

Bull's Eye: Make a full circle clockwise from the middle. Frame it by making the next circular stripe in the opposite direction. Continue to edge. Each pass in the pattern should erase the previous turn marks.

Plaid: Mow side-by-side parallel lines. Make crossing stripe lines at a 90-degree angle to the first set. Drive out on the previous light stripe, then mow coming back beside the last dark return stripe.

Star (right): This is a tricky pattern. To get a real feel for how something like a star will look, it's helpful to draw it out on paper first. That will also show you that the pattern's proportion is in scale to the site.

GREEN SOX Mellor and the rest of the Red Sox grounds crew had the field at Fenway Park in pristine shape with the team's socks logo and a checkerboard pattern during Game 2 of the 2007 Series.

BASEBALLS

EACH RAWLINGS BASEBALL USED IN RECENT FALL CLASSICS bears the World Series emblem in gold ink. Many of these specially marked balls are well traveled by the time Game 1 begins, as each of the four teams involved in League Championship Series play receives 30 dozen (360) official World Series balls. The losers of the ALCS and NLCS must hand over the baseballs to the winning teams at the conclusion of each best-of-seven series.

"You could look at it as adding insult to injury, but nobody looks at it as awkward," said Brian O'Gara, MLB's senior director of special events. "It's handled by the equipment managers and even though they clearly have a rooting interest, it's all part of the job to ensure we're prepared no matter where we end up for the World Series."

With 1,440 balls available for the event, there are more than enough for the games. Some are signed by the participating teams and earmarked for players, teams or the Commissioner's Office.

Fans who catch foul balls have the added thrill of receiving a specially marked keepsake. This isn't always the case for batting practice, however, when teams will often use regular-season balls.

BALL CLASSIC
An official 1993 Fall
Classic ball displays
the Series' logo.

GAME 2: THE FINISHING TOUCHES

PROGRAMS

PRICELESS COLLECTIBLES
Vendors sell programs at Citizens
Bank Park in Philadelphia before
Game 4 of the 2008 World Series.

THE OFFICIAL *WORLD SERIES PROGRAM* ISN'T JUST A GUIDE TO THE FALL Classic and the teams competing for the championship. It's a 200-plus-page keepsake with two dozen feature-length stories and 75,000 words that chronicle World Series and baseball history, as well as current Big League trends. The content is written by some of baseball's best writers, including Tim Kurkjian, Jayson Stark and Roger Kahn.

"It's critical that the *World Series Program* is as up-to-date as possible," said Don Hintze, MLB's vice president of publishing and photos, whose department is in charge of producing all of MLB's special-event programs. "By waiting until the World Series matchup is determined, we're able to feature players from each participating team on the cover, as well as a post-season recap, which highlights how each team advanced to the Fall Classic. That helps make the programs more valuable to fans."

The *World Series Program* debuted along with the Fall Classic in 1903. Then, each team produced a volume for its home games that contained rosters and local advertisements. Entrepreneur and Polo Grounds conces-sionaire Harry M. Stevens is credited with publishing more than one-third of all *World Series Programs* before MLB took over the responsibility in 1974.

Features of the modern book include a scorecard as well as two sections of either eight, 16 or 32 pages produced by the participating clubs. These local sections include rosters, short player profiles, season recaps, brief features and accounts of any previous Fall Classic appearances.

Mike McCormick, the editorial director for MLB, looks at the con-tending teams when assigning stories in August. In 2008, a story on first-time pennant contenders focusing on the Rays proved prescient when they advanced to the World Series. There are times, however, when a team like the 2007 Rockies comes out of nowhere late in the season, causing a last-minute scramble for content.

"The main goal is for this program to have a local feel when possible and an event feel so that no matter where it's held, you'll have several features on World Series history," said McCormick, who has worked on the *World Series Program* for more than a dozen years. "The history is important because that's what the event is all about."

As pages are produced at MLB's Manhattan offices beginning in Au-gust, they're sent to Quad Graphics' pre-press plant in New York. Proofs are then sent back to MLB for color correction and approval. The final product is then printed in the Quad Graphics facility in Sussex, Wis., and delivered by truck, or plane if necessary, to the cities hosting the Fall Classic. Cover art is designed for all four possible World Series matchups so that printing can commence as soon as the second LCS ends.

"The program is among the most highly collectible items associated with the event," said Hintze. "Not only does it contain information from some of the most renowned baseball writers of our generation, it's also the perfect keepsake. Many of our fans have programs collected from decades ago and always want to make sure their collection is updated. That's part of what makes the *World Series Program* so sought after — it's a timeless souvenir."

GAME 3: GAME TIME

WHETHER IT'S THE PATRIOTIC THRILL OF SEEING A SITTING U.S. PRESIDENT TOSS OUT the ceremonial first pitch, the pleasure of hearing a top-flight recording artist sing the national anthem, or the exhilaration of watching a cluster of fighter jets fly over the stadium, there is nothing quite like game day during the World Series. The pregame ceremonies energize the ballpark as the two teams competing for the crown prepare to take the diamond. With every blade of grass in its proper place on the field, every seat filled in the stands and a blimp perched high above the ballpark, there is all the pomp and pageantry that one would expect for such a storied event. Of course, one untimely rainstorm and everyone might have to try again the next day, but the flags, balloons and musicians are always ready to resume their places.

MILE HIGH Boston and Colorado participate in pregame ceremonies prior to Game 3 of the 2007 World Series at Coors Field.

LAST LICKS Mets outfielder Willie Mays takes batting practice in Oakland during the 1973 World Series; he retired after the seven-game Series concluded.

BATTING PRACTICE

Fans arriving early to a World Series game may be surprised to see a large crowd of people lingering on the field during batting practice, filling virtually all of the foul territory between the bases. Most of the people in the crowd are members of the media or officials from Major League Baseball and its clubs. Unlike the regular season, when there's far less media coverage of any one game and the clubhouses are open for three-hour stretches before contests, during the postseason the clubhouses are closed before games.

Without access to the clubhouse, the field becomes the only place for the media throng to congregate and gather information before the first pitch. Being able to watch the game's brightest stars take batting practice prior to a game is one of the nicer perks of covering baseball. Because of the sheer number of reporters on the field at this time, players and managers rarely stop for interviews. They know that if they answer one question they'll get mobbed and face a 20-minute free-for-all — all when they should be focusing on the contest ahead.

With players and managers mostly unavailable, the batting practice period is the best shot for reporters to interview general managers and front-office staff from the participating teams, along with officials from Major League Baseball, its television partners and the MLB Players Association. It's also the time when any celebrities or dignitaries attending the game might be allowed on the field.

Plus, with representatives from so many media outlets on hand, World Series batting practice is a prime networking opportunity. While reporters are there in the hopes that a major interview opportunity arises, one usually doesn't, and media members spend much of the time talking with each other, sharing ideas and anecdotes about the participating clubs.

PRACTICE MAKES PERFECT Fans at Fenway Park look on as the Boston Red Sox take batting practice before battling the New York Giants in the 1912 World Series.

FIRST COME, FIRST SERVED
With hordes of media and MLB
personnel on the field, early fans watch
the Astros warm up their bats before
Game 4 of the 2005 World Series.

FRONT AND CENTER
MLB Commissioner Bud Selig tries to keep warm as he watches Game 5 of the 1997 World Series in Cleveland.

COMMISSIONER'S BOX

O NE OF THE PERKS OF BEING C OMMISSIONER OF M AJOR L EAGUE B ASEBALL IS HAVING PRIME seats for the World Series. The game's top executive takes in the action during the Fall Classic from a section known as the commissioner's box. The so-called "box" refers to two locations. The first area is not so much a box as it is a three-row section of 15 to 20 seats per row, usually among the first rows between home plate and third base or home plate and first base, depending on the ballpark.

This VIP area is reserved for the commissioner and other high-ranking MLB officials, representatives from baseball's top business partners, owners of non-participating teams and, of course, celebrities. Some of the big names are in attendance to promote new films or television projects, whereas others are simply big fans of the participating teams.

"They tend to come out of the woodwork for the World Series since it's such a happening," said Marla Miller, MLB's senior vice president for special events.

MLB provides television producers with the seat locations of the commissioner and other notable guests in case the network wants to put anyone on camera for the audience at home. Images of the commissioner watching the World Series bundled up in an overcoat date back to Kenesaw Mountain Landis, the first man to hold the job. But for many baseball fans, the enduring image is of Bowie Kuhn from Game 2 of the 1976 World Series in Cincinnati, where the fifth commissioner of baseball sat in a front-row box without an overcoat despite the frigid weather.

Kuhn, who in 1971 had made the then-controversial decision to switch World Series games from afternoon to night, went without an overcoat to show that cool nighttime weather in autumn was of little concern to players and fans. His image was broadcast to viewers across the country and helped establish the tradition of night baseball during the Fall Classic.

But nowadays the commissioner does have the option of getting out of the cold and heading inside to a luxury suite, reserved as the second commissioner's box. Seating between 15 and 20 people, it allows the commissioner to confer privately with baseball officials.

The suite also provides privacy for celebs and dignitaries who might not want to sit in the stands. When Hank Aaron and Vera Clemente, the widow of Roberto Clemente, are on hand for the presentation of the Hank Aaron Award and Roberto Clemente Award, respectively, they'll often sit in the suite, as will the Commissioner's wife.

Like other MLB employees, Commissioner Bud Selig is working during each World Series game. At the very least, he's speaking informally with team owners, sponsors, local politicians and members of the media. Generally there isn't pressing business to be discussed during the game, but it's a possibility, and the Commissioner must be prepared for any situation that may arise, on or off the field.

The Commissioner's security detail will assist him with getting to his seats and moving between the field-level box and the luxury suite during the game. At least once during each World Series, Selig appears on the field during batting practice to speak with the media.

"He's pulled in so many directions during the World Series," said Earnell Lucas, MLB's vice president of security and facility management. "He has a full day on his hands."

Images of the commissioner watching the World Series bundled up in an overcoat date back to Kenesaw Mountain Landis, the first man to hold the job. For many baseball fans, the enduring image is of Bowie Kuhn from Game 2 of the 1976 World Series in Cincinnati.

ANTHEMS

THE WORLD SERIES IS MORE THAN JUST A GRAND STAGE FOR MAJOR League Baseball's two best teams. For top musical talent, it's a chance to perform the national anthem in front of a huge audience. Not surprisingly, the Fall Classic brings out some of the biggest names in music. The goal, according to MLB's Marla Miller, senior vice president for special events, is to award the assignment to a performer with national appeal and, ideally, a connection to the city that is hosting that particular game.

Performers tapped for the prestigious honor have ranged from former *American Idol* contestants Carrie Underwood and Clay Aiken to stars who appeal to an even younger generation, like Taylor Swift. Classic artists have certainly belted out *The Star-Spangled Banner* on the World Series stage as well, with Patti LaBelle, James Taylor, Gloria Estefan, Melissa Etheridge, Billy Joel and Paul Simon being just a few of the names that have performed prior to the first pitch of the ballgame. Artists range from many genres of music, too, with country artists, rockers and, yes, even boy bands getting the chance to take center stage.

The selection of national anthem singers begins well in advance of the World Series. In mid-September, contending teams submit to MLB a list of performers who have an affinity for the team or a connection to the community. Some musical acts can perform only in certain cities on specific dates because of scheduling conflicts, but performers are usually honored to sing the anthem. For Games 5 through 7, MLB does not release the names of anthem singers until it's determined that such games will be necessary.

There's always the possibility of a last-minute change due to unforeseen circumstances. Before Game 5 of the 2008 World Series in Philadelphia, Daryl Hall of the band Hall & Oates came down with the flu. Hall, a Pennsylvania native and graduate of Temple University, turned to his longtime singing partner John Oates to pinch-hit. Oates, who did not get the call at his Colorado home until 8 a.m. the morning of Game 5, scrambled to make it to Philadelphia, just 25 miles from where he grew up in North Wales, Pa.

Except in those rare, last-minute-change situations, performers complete a rehearsal, generally around 1 p.m., to gauge their comfort level in the stadium, and also to give MLB officials an idea of how long the rendition of the anthem will last. This enables the TV network to plan the length of its pregame commercial break, hopefully down to the second. The rehearsals also help set the timing for things like flyovers and fireworks.

Performers typically arrive at the ballpark with managers, agents or other handlers. Major League Baseball also provides staffers and resident security agents to help the acts travel around the park smoothly. Anthem singers receive World Series-themed clothing and other souvenirs, and many stay for the game.

"You'll find that top-tier musical talent is always interested because of the promotional value and exposure," Miller said. "No matter how successful they are, it's not every day you get a chance to perform at the World Series."

CLASSIC Ray Charles performs prior to Game 2 of the 2001 World Series.

STARS AND STRIPES Carrie Underwood sings the national anthem prior to Game 3 of the 2007 World Series at Coors Field.

FLYOVERS

NOTHING ADDS DRAMA AND PAGEANTRY TO A MAJOR SPORTING event quite like a carefully executed military flyover following the singing of the national anthem. To commemorate an event as grand as the World Series, Major League Baseball works with the U.S. military to provide flyovers for the Fall Classic, although poor weather conditions and logistical issues, such as close proximity to an airport, can sometimes prove to be challenging.

Under guidelines established by the Department of Defense, the secretaries of each branch of the armed services determine which events may receive flyovers. MLB, like other professional sports leagues requesting flyovers, must stipulate that the event in question is open to the public, non-political in nature and not a fundraiser for any particular charity.

The military pays for flyovers, which count as training flights for pilots and thus come out of existing budgets. In return, the military receives exposure for recruiting. MLB also provides tickets to the flight crews, along with World Series souvenirs. Later in the game, the pilots are shown on the in-game video monitors and often on the TV broadcast as well.

"We always try to have a flyover for the first home game in each city," said Marla Miller, MLB's senior vice president for special events. "It's just a question of the logistical circumstances we're facing, where the stadium is and weather patterns."

The U.S. Navy's Blue Angels — who have performed aerial demonstrations since 1946 — handle many big-event flyovers, although Miller said MLB also receives requests from the U.S. Army and Air Force. MLB's security department works with the FAA for air clearance in the vicinity of the stadium. Because of the noise generated by the aircraft as they pass over the stadium, clubs make an announcement and show the incoming aircraft on the scoreboard video monitor to prepare fans. Even when fully prepared, the flyover can be breathtaking.

Although post-9/11 security measures prohibit blimps from flying directly over stadiums while shooting footage for the TV broadcast of the World Series, the military faces no such restrictions when executing flyovers. In some respects, airspace is less crowded now than it was prior to 9/11, when small planes pulling advertising frequently circled World Series ballparks.

TOP GUNS Air Force fighters fly over Pacific Bell Park (now AT&T Park) before Game 3 of the 2002 World Series between the Angels and Giants.

PAGEANTRY Coors Field celebrates the Rockies' first Fall Classic appearance in 2007, as jets fly above the crowd (top left corner).

MOTHER NATURE

WHILE IT'S IMPOSSIBLE TO CONTROL THE WEATHER, MAJOR League Baseball does its best to be prepared for anything that Mother Nature has to offer. Each of baseball's 30 ballparks has a mini weather station installed high in the grandstands that transmits information to the Maryland headquarters of WeatherBug, a national forecasting service.

WeatherBug sends these reports to Jimmie Lee Solomon, MLB's executive vice president of baseball operations, who pays particular attention to the data toward the end of the season as the weather grows cooler in much of the country. MLB also crosschecks the information against other forecasting services, and some teams even enlist the help of their own local weather services.

When the World Series begins, MLB officials have a good idea of the prevailing weather patterns in the two host cities. They're aware of any "bands" of bad weather coming toward the ballparks and how they might impact the games. Before Game 5 of the 2008 World Series in Philadelphia, MLB officials knew of rain advancing toward the city but believed there was a long enough window to play the game. Unfortunately, the storm arrived sooner than expected, and the game had to be suspended after the top of the sixth inning amid torrential downpours.

"Sometimes it's the roll of the dice, even when you have the best information," said Solomon. "We put a lot of resources into this, but weather can be very unpredictable, even for the experts."

Although 2008 saw the first suspended game in World Series history, weather often has a way of making itself relevant. The Fall Classic has experienced more than 20 postponements because of rain. Although the weather has mostly cooperated in recent decades, there have been a few exceptions. Prior to '08, Game 4 of the 2006

Fall Classic was delayed a day in St. Louis due to rain. Game 1 of the 1996 World Series at Yankee Stadium was pushed back a day because of inclement weather. Fans had to wait a day for Game 7 at Shea Stadium in 1986, following the epic Game 6 between the Mets and Red Sox. Rain also delayed Game 6 of the 1981 World Series in New York between the Yankees and Dodgers.

In 1975, Game 6 of the Red Sox-Reds Series was postponed for three days in Boston. That turned out to be the game Carlton Fisk won with a 12th-inning homer down the left-field line at Fenway Park to force Game 7.

The 1962 World Series between the Yankees and Giants saw two rain postponements. Game 5 in New York was pushed back one day, while Game 6 in San Francisco was postponed three times as torrential downpours pelted the West Coast.

Game 4 of the 1911 World Series between the New York Giants and Philadelphia A's was delayed a whopping six days.

With newer ballparks being erected all around the league, World Series rainouts are less of a threat because of new technologies that provide for faster-draining fields. Retractable roofs also minimize the threat of washouts, as do baseball's few remaining domed stadiums.

When weather becomes an issue during a World Series, Solomon and his staff confer with the general managers and managers of the participating teams. The umpires and groundskeepers are involved. Commissioner Bud Selig, however, makes the final decision on delays and postponements.

"The overwhelming concern and desire is to get the game in, with the understanding that you want the conditions safe for players and fans," Solomon said. "You ultimately have to make a decision and it becomes dicey. Mother Nature doesn't always cooperate."

SILVER LININGS

A rain delay during the World Series can cause problems for fans who have traveled to the host city, television networks that scheduled the broadcast, and many other people working behind the scenes at the Fall Classic. But if rain comes at the right time it can be a blessing for the players and managers vying for the world championship. An unanticipated off day provides weary athletes with extra rest and sometimes allows managers the option of bringing back a top pitcher earlier than expected.

On Oct. 18, 1975, the Red Sox were trailing the Reds in the World Series, 3 games to 2, when the skies opened above Boston, postponing Game 6 for 72 hours. The delay allowed Boston to send Luis Tiant back to the mound when Game 6 took place on Oct. 21. Tiant had notched complete-game wins in Games

1 and 4. Although Carlton Fisk's arm-waving heroics remain the lasting image from that game, it was Tiant's eight innings of work that kept the Sox alive long enough for Fisk to deliver his game-winning blow in the 11th.

During the 1911 World Series between the New York Giants and the Philadelphia A's, an unprecedented one-week rain delay enabled Giants skipper John McGraw to start pitcher Christy Mathewson in back-to-back games. After winning a pitchers' duel with Chief Bender in Game 1, New York's ace took the loss in Game 3. Thanks to the torrential rains in the northeast, though, Mathewson was able to toe the rubber again at the start of Game 4. Alas, his opponent, Chief Bender, was even better rested — having not pitched since Game 1 — and notched the win for Philly.

RAIN DANCE Players and fans at Busch Stadium in St. Louis wait through a postponement during Game 4 of the 2006 World Series.

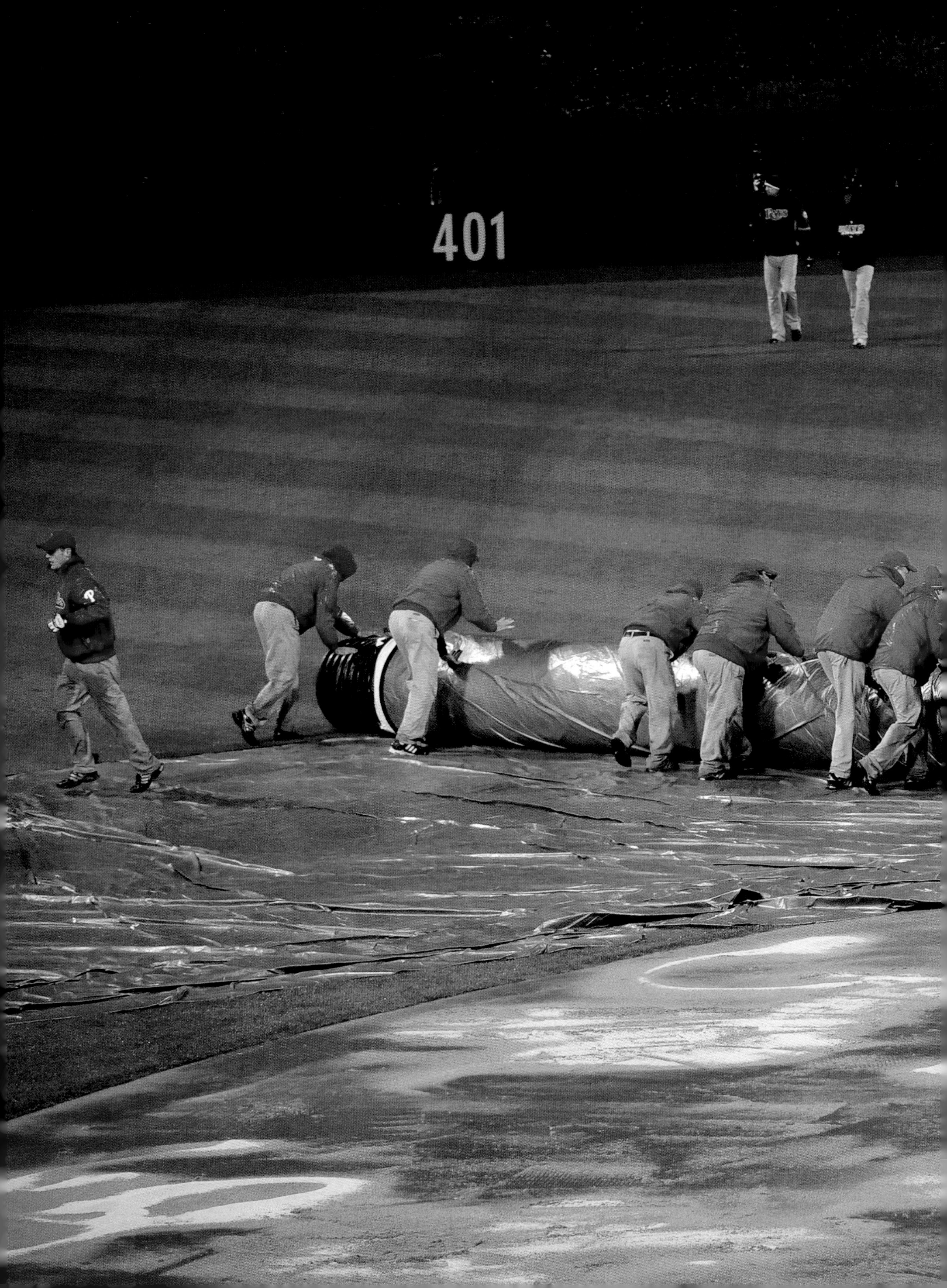
401

REIGN DELAY The Phillies grounds crew covers the field with a tarp during the decisive Game 5 in 2008, which was suspended for two days due to rain.

GAME 3: GAME TIME

FIRST PITCH

HONORED President George W. Bush throws out the ceremonial first pitch before Game 3 of the 2001 World Series at Yankee Stadium.

THE MOST DRAMATIC CEREMONIAL FIRST PITCH IN WORLD SERIES history came on Oct. 30, 2001. Less than two months after the 9/11 terrorist attacks, President George W. Bush took the field at Yankee Stadium prior to Game 3 amid unprecedented security.

Unlike most ceremonial first pitchers, Bush stood atop the mound, not closer to the plate. That may have been prompted by some friendly ribbing from Yankees shortstop Derek Jeter, who warned the President: "This is New York. If you throw from the base of the mound, they're going to boo you."

President Bush was the first sitting president to deliver a World Series first pitch since Dwight D. Eisenhower in 1956. Wearing a bullet-proof vest under his jacket, he delivered a strike to Yankees backup catcher Todd Greene as chants of "U-S-A, U-S-A" rang out through the House That Ruth Built.

The process of choosing someone for the ceremonial first pitch begins during the regular season. In mid-September, contending teams submit a list of potential pitchers to Major League Baseball. The list includes prominent local politicians and celebrities, former players and team owners and retired baseball legends that live in the area.

These days, the first pitch is really the second pitch. The first pitch, which is not filmed for television, is made by a representative of one of Major League Baseball's top sponsors or a winner of a sponsor sweepstakes. It's a low-key part of the ceremony, but one that has become quite important.

"Our goal is to give the fans and our various business partners access to the World Series in unique ways," said Tim Brosnan, MLB's executive vice president for business. "We want to accomplish that without causing a single bit of distraction to the two clubs that are competing."

Aside from the first pitches, pregame ceremonies also include the delivery of the game ball to the mound, which is often done by a local VIP. It could be someone affiliated with the host club, or someone who has made a great impact in the local community.

For Game 3 of the 2008 World Series in Philadelphia, the Phillies and Major League Baseball invited country music star Tim McGraw as a symbolic gesture to honor his late father, Tug McGraw. The elder McGraw pitched the Phillies to a World Series win in 1980 and was the last pitcher to close a Fall Classic win for the team until Brad Lidge in '08.

Unlike preparations for the national anthem, there's no on-field rehearsal for those tossing out the first pitch, although honorees can warm up in the batting cages beneath the stadium. It's not uncommon for fans to good naturedly boo a poor throw.

"Many of the people chosen are former players, at least at some level," said Marla Miller, senior vice president for special events. "It's a tremendous honor that people seem to be well prepared for, especially at the World Series."

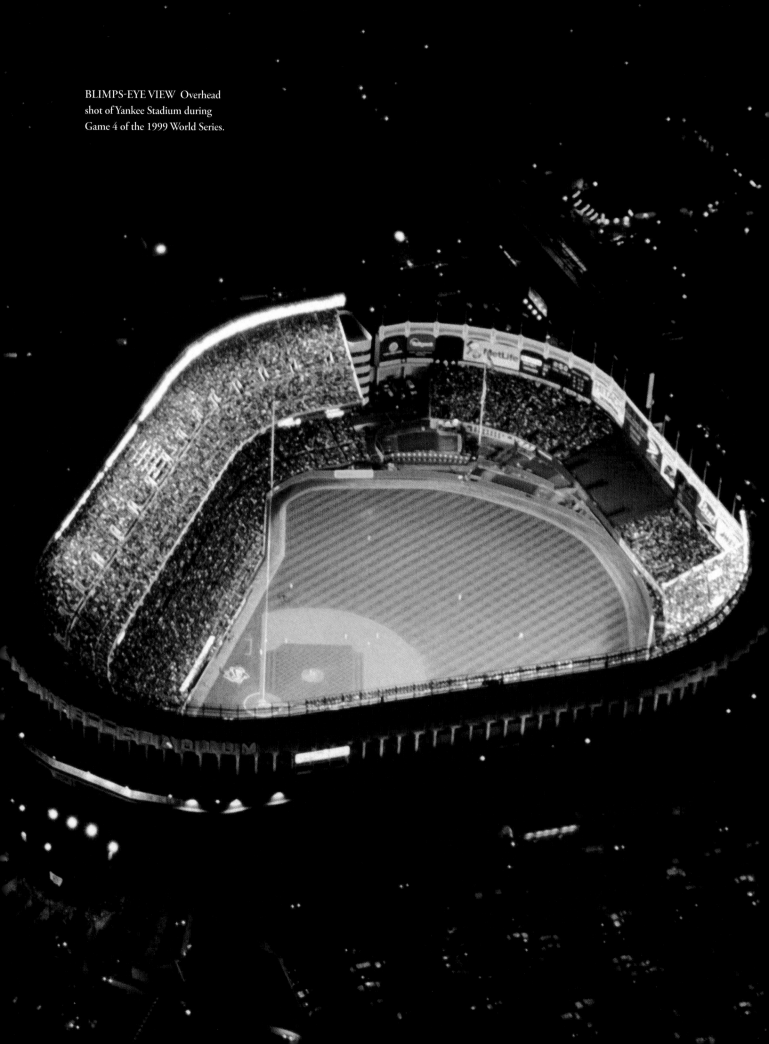

BLIMPS-EYE VIEW Overhead
shot of Yankee Stadium during
Game 4 of the 1999 World Series.

OVERHEAD VIEW

NO WORLD SERIES IS COMPLETE WITHOUT A BLIMP CIRCLING overhead, adding to the on-site fanfare of the event with eye-in-the-sky camera shots.

"The shot gives the broadcast a big-event feel," said Jerry Steinberg, Fox Sports' vice president of field and technical operations. "Even if it's a domed stadium, you still get the shots of the city, the traffic and the lights of the dome."

The famous Goodyear blimp has made multiple World Series appearances, but the star of the 2007 and 2008 Fall Classics was a blimp emblazoned with the logo of DirecTV, one of the satellite television providers that has carried MLB's Extra Innings package.

Blimps were pioneered by Goodyear and came to prominence during World War II as escort ships, spotting German U-boats from the air. But their involvement in sports goes back further, according to Goodyear spokesman Ed Ogden.

The company's first blimp — *Pilgrim* — made an appearance at the 1925 World Series pitting Washington against Pittsburgh. The first use of a blimp in a sports broadcast came in 1960 when CBS producer Frank Chirkinian was looking for a different camera shot of the Orange Bowl in Miami. Soon, blimps were commonplace at major sports events.

"People just love these big happy balloons in the sky," said Robert Mercer, a DirecTV spokesman who previously worked for Goodyear. "We sometimes refer to them as 'gregarious gasbags.'"

The helium-filled airships hover just 1,500 feet above the ground, providing stunning images from cameras specifically positioned for sports broadcasts.

Until recently, advertisers provided the blimps free of charge to the television network in exchange for several appearances during the broadcast, so-called "in-and-out" shots either before or after a commercial break.

That arrangement has evolved in recent years, according to Pete Macheska, the coordinating producer for MLB on Fox. The television network now tries to get companies to commit to blimp deals as part of larger advertising packages involving commercial spots.

Perhaps the most dramatic deployment of a blimp came during the 1989 World Series between the Oakland A's and San Francisco Giants. The Goodyear blimp *Columbia* was providing lead-up, aerial coverage for Game 3 when the Loma Prieta earthquake struck just as the television broadcast began.

While virtually all local electrical power was knocked out and local television operations were interrupted, the *Columbia* flew over San Francisco providing coverage of the destruction for multiple news organizations. The airship also provided emergency information on its electronic sign and emergency response teams began using the blimp's television pictures to direct their rescue crews to the hardest hit areas.

The DirecTV *HD Starship*, like most airships, is operated by the Lightship Group, a Florida company that operates almost all of the blimps in Europe and the United States, with the exception of the three Goodyear blimps.

The DirecTV model is an A-170LS Lightsign Lightship that features a giant 30-by-70 foot lighted screen to display messages and interact with fans. The blimp is 178 feet long, 46 feet wide, 55 feet tall and holds 170,000 cubic feet of helium.

The passenger cabin, called the gondola, is 11.4 feet long, 5 feet wide and over 6 feet tall. That's barely enough room for four adults and the pilot. Despite the close quarters, and since it's not available to the public, a blimp ride is a treat. Only crew members, those associated with the sponsor, and an occasional member of the media get to enjoy the unusual vantage point.

Since blimps are capable of safely cruising at a speed of 35 to 40 miles per hour and cannot be transported unless they are in flight, it can be a challenge for a blimp to appear at both World Series venues unless the sites are within a manageable distance. The DirecTV blimp debuted in Boston at the 2007 World Series, appeared at Yankee Stadium for the All-Star Game in '08 and then made it to Philadelphia for the '08 World Series. The decision to not try and make the arduous ride back and forth between Philadelphia and St. Petersburg during the '08 Classic was simple since Tropicana Field is a domed ballpark and in-game shots are not possible.

> The first use of a blimp in a sports broadcast came in 1960 when CBS was looking for a different camera shot of the Orange Bowl in Miami. Soon, blimps were commonplace at major sports events.

Blimps are regulated by the same Federal Aviation Administration (FAA) regulations as other aircraft. Since 9/11, they have not been allowed to fly directly above stadiums, which has limited the ways in which they can be used during the television broadcasts. Prior to 2001, the blimps were used for panoramic shots of the host city and the ballpark as well as for catching the action on the field. Safety restrictions currently prevent them from doing the latter.

"If you want to do replay shots, you need them above the stadium," said Macheska. "Otherwise you're kind of limited to just scene and beauty shots."

EYE IN THE SKY The Goodyear blimp flies over the lights at Oakland-Alameda County Coliseum during the 1988 World Series.

WINE AND DINE St. Petersburg's Renaissance Vinoy Hotel provided a picturesque setting for the Rays' gala prior to Game 1 of the 2008 World Series.

TIME TO TOAST

It was the night before Game 1 of the 2008 World Series and Jamie Moyer strolled poolside at the Renaissance Vinoy Hotel in St. Petersburg, mingling among Major League Baseball sponsors and officials from the host Tampa Bay Rays and his Philadelphia Phillies. Although players generally don't attend the official World Series galas — held on the evenings before the first game in each participating city — the Phillies, coincidentally, were staying at the Vinoy, which made it easy for Moyer to drop by.

Even for professional athletes and others accustomed to upscale events, World Series galas are impressive affairs. Usually held at a high-end resort or famous civic attraction, they give each participating club and MLB's extended business community the opportunity to celebrate the Fall Classic.

Major League Baseball provides the participating postseason teams with a Hospitality Allowance for the party, and teams can augment the allowance if they wish. About 2,500 invitations are extended to each of the two galas. The host team invites its sponsors, broadcast partners and local retail accounts. The entire front office is invited, along with members of the opposing team's traveling party. Media covering the Fall Classic are invited, and MLB extends invites to sponsors and dignitaries in town for the event. Invites also go out to political leaders, as well as other baseball people located nearby, including members of local Minor League organizations.

Waiters circulate, offering hors d'oeuvres, while guests can enjoy an open bar. There's usually a baseball-themed ice sculpture standing sentry above a buffet of gourmet food.

Plans for a gala cannot be confirmed until a club advances to the World Series, so they sometimes are put together in as few as two days. Since teams cannot fully commit to destinations in advance, they sometimes lose out on popular sites. When the Chicago White Sox reached the World Series in 2005, many of the Windy City's most popular venues were booked, but the White Sox still were able to host a memorable event at the historic Palmer House Hilton.

In 2002, the Angels, owned at the time by the Disney Company, hosted their gala at Disneyland. The Braves once used the World of Coca-Cola, the Coke-themed museum in Atlanta. Memorable New York venues have included Tavern on the Green in Central Park and Vanderbilt Hall at Grand Central Terminal. The Boston Red Sox have used the JFK Museum and the Florida Marlins have hosted friends and partners at the lavish Fairmont Turnberry Isle Resort & Club.

In addition to the galas, the two teams often stage pregame and post-game parties, either in a club area of the ballpark or, in warmer locales, outside under large tents. Invites go out to the same lists of people as for the gala, providing even more opportunities for baseball's extended business community to celebrate the game's showcase event.

A WORLD SERIES DAY IN THE LIFE OF AN MLB CLUB'S GALA PLANNER

Joseph W. Giles is the director of business development for the Philadelphia Phillies and planned the gala held before Game 3 of the 2008 World Series.

8 a.m.: Arrive at the ballpark; distribute invitations internally and to MLB guests, media members, etc. Check with the gala planning team on setup, band, caterer, parking, gifts, decorations, security, etc.

10 a.m.: Allocate and distribute parking passes for gala to Phillies staff and guests. Answer phone calls with questions about the gala (all day long).

11 a.m.–12p.m.: Drive to site of gala; check on progress of setup. Then return to ballpark.

12–1 p.m.: Check on gala party favors to see that they have been safely delivered to site. Get something to eat for lunch.

1–2 p.m.: Review last-minute details with caterer; update list of attendees, including VIPs; discuss setup and decorations at site of gala.

2–3 p.m.: Confirm that outside private security force is working with club's own security officials and that the evening's plans are finalized.

3–5 p.m.: Depart office and check in at hotel near site of gala.

5–5:30 p.m.: Arrive at site of gala; supervise last-minute setup at site.

5:30–6 p.m.: Return to hotel; shower and dress for festivities.

6–6:45 p.m.: Return to gala, conduct meeting with all staff and send everyone to appropriate stations.

6:45 p.m.: Open doors at site; greet invited guests as they arrive.

7 p.m.–12 a.m.: Circulate throughout the gala, checking with guests about food, beverages and music. Deal with any problems as they arise.

12 a.m.: Gala ends. Clear out guests; close site.

1:30 a.m.: Return to hotel.

GAME 4: COVERING THE SERIES

THE FALL CLASSIC IS UNDOUBTEDLY SHAPED BY THE PLAYERS AND MANAGERS WHO vie for the crown. But the ways that we remember each World Series are shaped by another group of hardworking professionals in attendance at each and every game. Crammed into crowded mid-level press boxes and in the field-level camera wells are thousands of men and women whose words and images help to paint the picture of each World Series. Their insights and dedication put each game in its proper perspective, which is no easy task given the event's rich history. Backed by public relations staffers from MLB and the participating clubs, the media members record each athletic feat and inspirational quote. All of this must happen so that the stories and photographs appearing in the morning paper — not to mention blogs, online publications and television broadcasts — are worthy of the games they chronicle.

ON THE JOB Media members report from a Yankee Stadium press box during the 1960 World Series between the Yankees and Pirates.

PUBLIC RELATIONS

IT'S ALL HANDS ON DECK FOR MAJOR LEAGUE BASEBALL'S public relations staff during the World Series. Almost the entire MLB 15-person PR staff travels from New York to the World Series sites to work press conferences and assist media members in multiple packed press boxes and press rooms. The group also distributes credentials and assists with any issues that unexpectedly arise. These can include spotty wireless Internet service in the press box, keeping certain elevators reserved for media use, or simply directing traffic in the post-game clubhouses.

The PR staff also handles the needs of national broadcast crews, some of which arise right after the last out of each game. MLB assigns a PR staffer to each of baseball's broadcast rights holders — television, radio, satellite radio, MLB International, MLB.com, MLB Network and MLB Productions. At the end of each game, the PR official helps locate players for post-game interviews.

In conjunction with the contingent from MLB, several team PR directors work the World Series most every year — a group that has included Rob Butcher of the Cincinnati Reds, Jay Horwitz of the New York Mets and Mike Herman of the Minnesota Twins.

Given the long hours PR directors put in from the start of Spring Training until the end of the regular season, working the World Series when your club doesn't even make it might seem like going beyond the call of duty. But the World Series workload isn't nearly as hectic for PR officials from eliminated teams as it is for the staffs of the clubs that make it to the Fall Classic.

Eighteen-hour days are common for the half-dozen-member PR staffs of the participating clubs. Each team also hires about a dozen college students to serve as "runners," distributing press notes and news conference transcripts throughout the press boxes. The students are selected from local universities, usually ones that feature communications or sports management programs.

"If we need 10, we'll get 20 people interested," said Mike Teevan, Major League Baseball's manager of media relations. "The response is usually pretty overwhelming."

Other key contributors to the PR effort include National Baseball Hall of Fame President Jeff Idelson as well as Communications Director Brad Horn, who writes many of the press notes issued by MLB before and after each World Series game. Since the notes tend to place performances and milestones within the historic context of the Fall Classic, it's a natural role for a Hall of Fame official.

MLB's top PR officials, Senior Vice President Richard Levin, Vice President Patrick Courtney and Matt Bourne, vice president of business public relations, are on hand to assist Commissioner Bud Selig and other high-ranking officials from the Commissioner's Office.

Bourne and Dan Queen, who handle business public relations for MLB, answer any media questions about licensing, merchandise sales, marketing and sponsorship, although they're just as likely to locate the appropriate MLB official to address any other media queries in person.

Indeed, since the vast majority of MLB officials are on hand for the World Series, PR staff members usually don't need to serve as spokespeople. But they can still provide background information, which often is all that's needed.

"We all do a little bit of everything during the World Series," said Teevan. "With so many media working on so many different stories, it's our job to make sure things move along smoothly."

RENAISSANCE MAN

A veteran of 10 Fall Classics, where one of his duties has often been to locate and corral the World Series MVP, Rob Butcher knows the big event well. He began working Major League Baseball's jewel events to get a firsthand look at all their machinations. When it was his Reds' turn to host one, he wanted to be ready.

"Everyone should want to work the World Series," said Butcher, who has held the title of Cincinnati Reds director of media relations since 1997. "If you've never worked a World Series or an All-Star Game and your team hosts one, I think you'd be really surprised at the magnitude."

Butcher has been a virtual fixture at big events like the World Series, where he works closely with MLB's media relations staff. His experience eventually paved the way for another assignment. The PR man took time out of Reds Spring Training in 2006 — and did so again in 2009 — to ply his trade for Team USA in the World Baseball Classic. "The best thing that happened was at our team meeting [in 2006]," Butcher recalls.

"[General Manager] Bob Watson and [Executive Director, Chief Executive Officer] Paul Seiler of USA Baseball laid it out to the players. 'Do what he asks you to do and go where he asks you to go.' And they did." Butcher said he could not have asked for a more accommodating group than the 2006 Team USA, which included Ken Griffey Jr., Derek Jeter and Chase Utley. The team was eliminated in the tournament's second round, but Butcher went on to assist WBC officials with the semifinals and finals. By tournament's end, he could say without hesitation that he had worked the biggest of all baseball events. "It was a larger World Series," said Butcher. "It was perhaps as big an event as MLB has ever had."

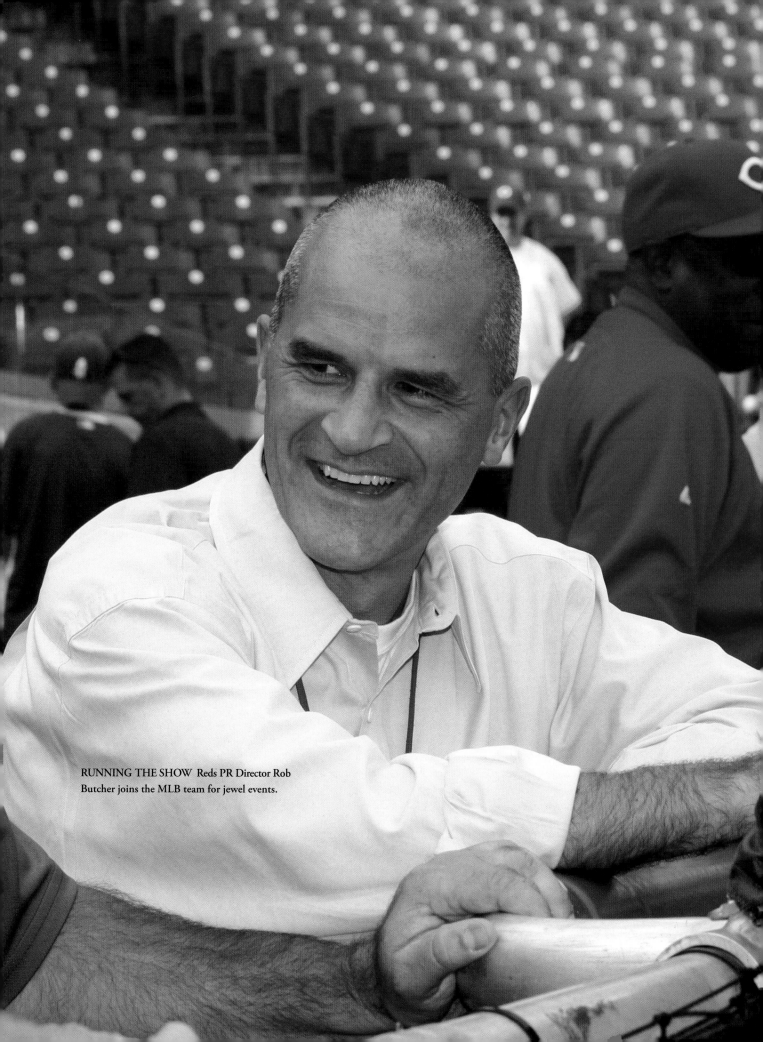

RUNNING THE SHOW Reds PR Director Rob Butcher joins the MLB team for jewel events.

PRESS BOX

SOME OF THE TOUGHEST SEATS TO ACQUIRE FOR THE WORLD SERIES are behind home plate — not just the seats in the first few rows, but also those in the mid-level press box.

With more than 2,000 media members representing all facets of communications — TV, print, radio, online — credentialed for the World Series, fewer than 10 percent of them can get a seat in the main press box. Most press boxes seat between 150 and 200 members of the media, more than sufficient space for the regular season but not for the playoffs or the World Series.

The Baseball Writers Association of America (BBWAA) determines which media outlets are given seats in the main press box. Those chosen are almost exclusively daily newspaper writers since they have the tightest deadlines and are most in need of quick access to the clubhouses.

Even then, not all writers from daily newspapers get a seat in the main box. The larger papers from the participating cities receive two or three seats apiece, filling front row spots as they do during the regular season when the team they cover is home. The Associated Press also gets at least two seats.

Larger daily newspapers such as *USA Today*, *The New York Times*, the *New York Post*, *The Philadelphia Inquirer*, the *Los Angeles Times* and *The Washington Post*, all of which have websites with special sports pages where information can appear immediately and sometimes exclusively, receive one seat apiece. The rest of their contingents, which for papers such as *USA Today* and *The New York Times* can be as many as five or six writers, are assigned to the auxiliary press box.

After that, the seats are allotted by rotation, with daily newspaper writers from several markets selected each year. This system gives most everyone a shot at a seat in the main box every few years. Several seats are reserved for public relations officials from both teams, along with several from MLB.

With every seat filled in the main box, it can get crowded. Some prefer to sit in the auxiliary press box, usually a converted section of outfield grandstands, or the working press room, which is usually carved out of a field-level storage area. For even more space, another working press area is often created out of the regular season's press dining room. But despite somewhat makeshift space, baseball writers treasure the opportunity to cover the game for a living and many have been on the job for years.

Fans often don't realize what a draining commitment covering a World Series is, and what long workdays these reporters put in during the postseason. Before the game starts, many writers will file "notebook" stories based on pregame interviews and any news learned before the game. They will then write a running account of the game that can be filed immediately after the last out. Once the game is over, they head downstairs, where the clubhouses open after a short cooling-off period, to interview players.

After getting quotes from available players, they hustle back upstairs to rewrite their game stories, inserting quotes and other information learned in the clubhouse, and often blogging. It's not uncommon for writers — who arrive at the ballpark hours prior to the first pitch — to be working at the ballpark for several hours after the game has ended.

A WORLD SERIES DAY IN THE LIFE OF A REPORTER

Steven Krasner covered the Red Sox for *The Providence (R.I.) Journal* from 1986 to 2008, reporting from the World Series in 1986, 2004 and 2007.

1:30–2 p.m.: Arrive at the ballpark; show credential at press gate; take elevator to mid-level press box; set up computer, media guides and other notes at assigned seat. Call office to confirm deadlines and assignments.

2–3 p.m.: Take elevator down to field level; mill about in front of dugouts with other media as players emerge for early stretching, hitting and fielding drills; join the scrum of reporters and cameramen approaching any player willing to answer questions.

3–4 p.m.: Go to interview room. The home manager will take questions for 15 minutes. After a short break, he will be followed by his team's next starting pitcher, the visiting manager and that manager's next starting pitcher.

4–5 p.m.: Return to press box to file — via blog — any interesting tidbits picked up while on the field or in the interview room.

5–7 p.m.: Return to field for batting practice. Join scrum around any players, managers or MLB executives granting interviews.

7–7:30 p.m.: Return to press box to blog any further facts or anecdotes learned during BP.

7:30–8 p.m.: Join other media members in press dining area.

8 p.m.–12 a.m.: View game from seat in press box; write throughout the contest and file updated stories at each of several deadlines.

12–12:30 a.m.: Once the game ends a reporter must choose whether to run down to the interview room or to head into the clubhouse. It is often best to head to the clubhouse to try to catch the players before all reporters with clubhouse credentials arrive.

1:30–2:30 a.m.: Return to press box. Revise previously filed stories to include quotes and materials that were unavailable earlier. Although the print editions are already closed, the online versions can be still be updated.

2:30 a.m.: Depart ballpark.

BEST SEAT IN THE HOUSE
A view from the press box at
Comiskey Park during the
1959 World Series.

VIEW FROM BELOW Fenway Park's enclosed press box prior to the start of Game 2 of the 2007 World Series.

GAME FACES Inside the press room before Game 2 of the 2008 World Series at Tropicana Field.

WATCHING THE ACTION Reporters fill in the "aux box" at Pacific Bell Park (now AT&T Park) in San Francisco during batting practice at the '02 Series.

AUXILIARY PRESS BOX

EVEN IN NEWER BALLPARKS, PRESS BOXES CAN'T SEAT MORE THAN 200 REPORTERS. THAT'S why teams must create auxiliary press boxes for the World Series and other big events, usually converting a section (or several sections) of seats into workspace. Teams hire local contractors to build workspaces, either by removing the seat backs in every other row of the "aux box" and bolting work stations to the base, or simply attaching work stations over those existing rows of seats.

In the days of multi-purpose stadiums, the auxiliary press box was often used for football, and tended to be larger since football teams draw more media during the regular season.

These days, the aux box is usually outside in a converted seating area. Security personnel are hired to stand at the entrances of the section. Television monitors are positioned throughout the area to show replays. Press notes and media updates are distributed by hired runners, and announcements made in the main press box can also be heard in the aux box.

During the 2008 World Series, the process was relatively easy at Tropicana Field, where three-quarters of a self-contained area known as the "TBT Party Deck" above left field was designated the auxiliary press box. With mostly bleacher seating, it was easy to convert. And since just one small seating area within the section remained for fans, the space almost felt like a private press area.

That's not always the case. In the former Yankee Stadium, which had a relatively small press box, journalists had to sit in an aux box converted from a section of seats beyond the outfield fence and in the upper deck. It wasn't a bad vantage point, but it placed the media in close proximity to Yankees fans.

Weather was an issue at Cleveland's Jacobs Field in 1995 and '97, where the aux box was a converted portion of the right-field stands. With temperatures hovering around freezing, it was too cold for reporters to type on laptops. Reporters that needed to write during the game were forced to take shelter in the field-level media room.

As recently as the early 1990s, before widespread use of laptops, the Internet and e-mail, the idea of sportswriters sitting in the stands and filing stories via telephone modem and primitive computers seemed like advanced technology. Media outlets had to incur the expense of installing telephone lines, both for story transmission and for reporters to communicate with their offices.

These days, World Series clubs provide wireless Internet service to the media members, who can e-mail stories to their offices. Some even file running blogs from the aux box during the game. Since reporters use cell phones to reach their offices, few telephone lines are installed in the aux box.

The aux boxes wipe out as many as a couple thousand seats in each World Series ballpark. Despite the loss of seats, Major League Baseball believes the additional media coverage adds to the grandeur of the World Series. Because fewer seats are available, World Series attendance figures usually rank among the ballparks' smallest sellouts.

Although the aux box could be viewed as second-class seating, many notable baseball journalists view the World Series from there, including most of the contingent from ESPN, *Sports Illustrated* and other national magazines. With technological advances, it's now more possible than ever to cover the game from anywhere in the ballpark.

> Although the aux box could be viewed as second-class seating, many notable baseball journalists view the World Series from there. With technological advances, it's now more possible than ever to cover the game from anywhere in the ballpark.

PRESS CREDENTIALS

WITH SEVERAL THOUSAND MEMBERS OF THE PRESS COVERING each World Series over the past decade, it's vital that proper credentials be issued. All members of the media, as well as anyone else working the event in an official capacity for Major League Baseball, are issued a laminated credential. This stringent process is for security purposes, but it also facilitates a productive working environment.

Anyone who has received press credentials to cover the World Series has passed muster with John Blundell, MLB's manager of media relations. He oversees credentials for all of baseball's jewel events. In addition to the World Series, the events range from the All-Star Game to the World Baseball Classic to MLB's Winter Meetings. It's definitely a demanding job. But the World Series — played in two cities over nearly two weeks — is perhaps the most hectic element.

About 2,000 press credentials are issued in each city for a typical Fall Classic, more if either New York team or the Boston Red Sox are involved. Many journalists cover games in both cities, although a portion of those based in the participating cities only attend home games. Either way, that's a lot of laminated passes. And it represents just a fraction of the applications received.

MLB prints the credentials at its Manhattan headquarters, using pre-laminated, watermarked cards. On the front of more recent credentials are the media member's name, affiliation and photo. The back includes fine-print warnings of the dangers of flying bats and balls and reminds journalists that autograph seeking is strictly prohibited.

A staff of six to 10 — a group of MLB and team officials — handles the distribution of credentials in each city. At the press gate, each media member presents identification and receives a credential, a lanyard to attach to the credential and wear around the neck, tickets to post-game gala receptions, and a press pin — one for each city.

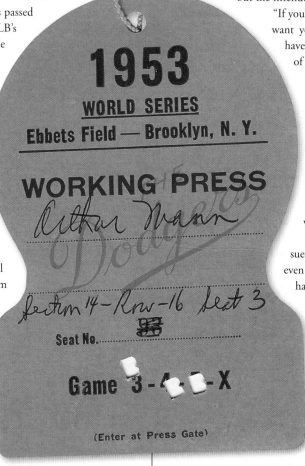

There is no memorabilia market for press passes, despite the fact that many media members retain their credentials as keepsakes from their careers.

With the advent of digital photography, Major League Baseball began to require that photos be submitted along with press credential applications. These passport-sized pictures are printed on the passes to ensure that they are not used by anyone but the intended person.

"If you're a legitimate media affiliation, we want you there," Blundell said. "But we have different guidelines for what kind of access you'll receive."

Since space in the clubhouse is limited, even in new ballparks with sprawling facilities, post-game access is capped at about 800 journalists who receive special clubhouse badges. There's a different badge in each city, although some journalists covering the entire postseason receive one for the whole period.

The number of credentials issued hasn't varied much in recent years even though the nature of the media has changed. There are fewer newspaper reporters than in the past, but there now are representatives from satellite radio, journalists from the many cable television channels, and those working in the ever-expanding world of online media.

With so many blogs and online baseball websites, MLB has to draw the line somewhere with credentials. Only those news organizations that have covered MLB through other mainstream media platforms receive access for their online reporters. This small group includes ESPN.com, Yahoo! Sports, CBS Sportsline and baseball's own MLB.com contingent.

As professional baseball rosters have become increasingly international, there has also been more interest from media outlets around the world. In 2008, MLB credentialed media from 23 countries, with Japan representing the largest contingent, on hand to chronicle Akinori Iwamura of the Tampa Bay Rays and So Taguchi of the Philadelphia Phillies.

PRESS CONFERENCES

DURING THE REGULAR SEASON, PLAYERS AND MANAGERS generally deal with members of the media in small group sessions that take place either in the clubhouse or in the dugout. But with more than 2,000 press credentials issued for the World Series every year, that often becomes impossible during the Fall Classic.

Those media members possessing clubhouse badges are still granted access to the clubhouses after games as they are during the regular season, but no one is allowed access to clubhouses before the contests.

To accommodate the heavy media demands before each World Series game, and to lessen the rush afterward, Major League Baseball creates a special interview room in the bowels

of each of the participating ballparks. Here, the managers and selected players are brought before reporters for question-and-answer sessions both before and after games.

The players and managers typically sit on a raised dais in front of a backdrop emblazoned with a pattern of official World Series and Major League Baseball logos. There's seating for about 200 reporters, and behind them is another raised platform positioned for television cameras.

Katy Feeney and Phyllis Merhige, both senior vice presidents of club relations for Major League Baseball, oversee the interview room and are the ones to call on reporters who have questions. Public relations interns roam the room with microphones so that

Q&A SESSION
Detroit Tigers Manager Jim Leyland gives a press conference prior to Game 3 of the 2006 World Series against the Cardinals at Busch Stadium.

the questions can be heard by the players and managers, as well as on the live video feeds, which are available to a variety of television networks around the country.

Feeney handles the National League team's press conferences and Merhige the American League, a tradition that goes back to when the leagues had separate offices. Veteran players and managers usually greet them with hugs upon approaching the dais.

The two executives make it a point to meet every team at the New York ballparks when they come into town during the regular season, but they also get to know them during the postseason by working various press conferences, starting with the Division Series.

"I always make the joke early on that they have to want to see a lot of me because I'll be there in October," Merhige said.

"If they're lucky, they'll be very sick of us by the end of the month," Feeney added.

Post-game press conferences have been staged for decades, but the pregame ritual dates back only to 1992, the year when Toronto Blue Jays Manager Cito Gaston asked if he could hold his pregame question-and-answer period in the interview room rather than subject himself to being swarmed on the field during batting practice. Soon both managers were regularly appearing in the interview room before games, along with the scheduled starting pitchers for the following day's game.

Merhige and Feeney skillfully move the process along in a timely manner, trying to get the first question asked as soon as the interviewees are seated. The paradox of the interview room is that in many cases reporters don't feel inclined to attend since transcripts are provided immediately afterward in the press boxes.

"Sometimes you worry that there won't be enough people there," Feeney said. "And there are times when you have to drag out the first couple of questions."

Tampa Bay Rays Manager Joe Maddon solved that problem during the 2008 World Series by assigning the first question at each of his press conferences to a local radio reporter, which continued a tradition that he began during the regular season.

Once each game concludes, public relations officials from each team escort the managers into the interview room. After they take their allotted cooling off period, the losing manager arrives first to avoid the potentially awkward situation of having to wait in the back of the room while the winning manager speaks.

Players from the losing team do not usually come to the interview room to take questions, preferring to speak back in the clubhouse, although high-profile players such as Roger Clemens and Randy Johnson have requested to do so in the past, in an attempt to avoid being swarmed at their lockers by a less-regulated group of media members.

The winning manager is next to appear on the dais and he is generally followed by one or two stars of the game. Those players will probably still face another barrage of interrogators once they make their way back to the clubhouse, but at least they've handled the initial onslaught in the interview room.

GLAD TO TALK Phillies hurler Cole Hamels and Manager Charlie Manuel happily talk with reporters during a press conference after defeating the Rays in five games to become World Series champions in 2008.

LOGGING THE INTERVIEWS

SOME REPORTERS DON'T BOTHER WRITING DOWN QUOTES AT World Series press conferences. That's because full transcripts are usually available by the time they return to the press box.

A New York company called ASAP Sports, founded in 1989 by former court reporter Peter Paul Balestrieri, provides instant transcripts at more than 150 major sporting events, including the World Series. ASAP Sports hires local court reporters in participating cities to sit in the front row and transcribe the press conferences.

Ozzie Guillen, who managed in the 2005 World Series and one other postseason, makes it a point to warn transcribers about his thick accent and tendency to talk fast. But not even Guillen presents much of a challenge for the seasoned court reporters, who can transcribe at least 260 words per minute. Rosters of both teams are pre-programmed into the reporters' special keyboards to prevent spelling mistakes. The transcripts are sent instantly via wireless Internet connection to the laptop of a nearby MLB official, who double-checks other baseball names.

The transcripts are subsequently photocopied and distributed to reporters, many of whom are working on deadline. Some journalists, both at the ballpark and off-site, receive them via e-mail. The transcripts also are published on the ASAP Sports Web site as well as on MLB's official website for media information.

The transcripts are a godsend for writers covering the Series, who often must spend precious time on deadline transcribing audio files from their digital recorders. The press-room transcripts represent just a portion of their interviews, along with those conducted around the batting cage before games and in the post-game clubhouse. But any time saved from transcribing is appreciated.

PRESS NOTES

WITH MORE THAN 100 YEARS OF HISTORY, THE WORLD SERIES generates a staggering amount of trivia and statistics, much of which is chronicled in press notes that are printed and distributed to members of the media before and after each game.

The participating teams each issue four to six pages of their own notes for each game, just as they do during the regular season. The cover sheet focuses on upcoming postseason-related milestones for the team or individual players, along with other pertinent facts that might not be evident to avid baseball fans.

The 2008 Tampa Bay Rays, for instance, were bidding to become just the fifth market to win a World Series, Super Bowl and Stanley Cup. Had they done so, they would have joined Boston, New York, Chicago and Pittsburgh.

The second page is dedicated to that day's starting pitcher, with a breakdown of all of his starts since Opening Day. Particular emphasis is placed on his performance during the postseason and in past matchups against his World Series opponent.

The third page gives info on bullpen members and their recent performances, streaks and trends. The final page goes to hitters, with focus on recent at-bats, key hits and noteworthy field stats.

The team-issued press notes tend to be shorter than they are during the regular season, as clubs put out voluminous postseason media guides once they reach the Division Series and also because Major League Baseball issues its own daily notes.

MLB's notes place each game in historical context. Before Game 2, there will be plenty of research on how the team that has won Game 1 has fared in the past. The Elias Sports Bureau, which provides historical research and statistical services for professional sports leagues, is a big help here. Elias noted, for example, that Game 1 of the 2008 World Series was just the third time that a Fall Classic had opened with starters who were both under the age of 25 (Cole Hamels of the Phillies and Scott Kazmir of the Rays).

The MLB notes also include a list of "featured guests," which includes the National Anthem singer, the person throwing out the ceremonial first pitch, and the seventh-inning "God Bless America" performer. The television ratings for the previous night's broadcast also are listed and placed in historical context.

The notes also provide housekeeping details, such as player and manager interview schedules for the following day. This sort of information allows the media to plan their schedules accordingly.

Once the game is over, MLB quickly issues a one-page sheet of noteworthy accomplishments, milestones and trivia from the completed game. Team interns and "runners" hired by MLB walk the aisles of the press boxes distributing the notes.

PRESSING QUESTIONS
Chicago White Sox Manager
Ozzie Guillen talks with
media before Game 4 of the
2005 World Series against
the Houston Astros at
Minute Maid Park.

THE PERFECT ANGLE Cameramen line
up to photograph Game 1 of the World
Series between Boston and Colorado at
Fenway Park in 2007.

SNAPSHOTS

From Yogi Berra's leap into the arms of Don Larsen in 1956 to Kirk Gibson's arm-pumping imitation of Oakland's Dennis Eckersley in 1988 to Joe Carter's bouncing home run trot in 1992, the World Series has produced a wealth of iconic images since the inaugural event more than a hundred years ago.

Not surprisingly, many news organizations want to be perfectly in position, ready to photograph those spontaneous moments when they occur. As a result, the field-level space in camera "wells" are premium spots during World Series games, and with so many reporters and photographers to begin with, things can get a little crowded.

A typical regular season game will usually attract just eight to 10 still photographers, who position themselves in the wells, which are sunken areas adjacent to the dugouts. During the World Series, though, that number can swell to more than 100, especially in recent years as top Japanese stars such as Hideki Matsui, Daisuke Matsuzaka and Akinori Iwamura have starred in the Fall Classic.

Photographers are assigned positions in the camera wells during the World Series by Rich Pilling, MLB's director of photography. Along with allocating spots in the photo wells, Pilling coordinates a team of three MLB photographers. One is stationed along the first-base line, another is planted along the third-base line and the third is perched above the field to capture overhead images.

"You never know where the photo is going to happen," said Pilling about shooting the Fall Classic. "I make sure to cover all possible angles with our photographers."

In the same way that participating teams need to construct auxiliary press boxes to accommodate all of the additional journalists on hand for the World Series, they also often construct additional space for photographers, which is usually located in small boxes along the first- and third-base lines, for ideal positioning during exciting moments.

Priority space in the main photo wells is designated for the wire services covering the event, such as The Associated Press, as well as local and regional newspapers of the participating teams and a wide range of magazines with national presence. In some instances, photographers end up stationing themselves in the stands — sometimes even in the auxiliary press boxes — to catch different angles of the action.

But even for photogs who shoot with long telephoto lenses, that's not an ideal position. Photographers who represent the same news organizations will often work together, strategically trading spots at various points during the game, so that they each have an opportunity to shoot at close range.

During the action-packed postseason, the most memorable shots often come during walk-off wins or during the initial celebration that occurs following the final out of the Series. In those instances, which happen suddenly and with unimaginable emotion, it is undoubtedly best for photographers to be up close.

The emergence of digital photography over the last decade or so has certainly revolutionized the logistics of sports photography. Before digital options, news organizations who were shooting "live" — for publication immediately — had to go through the procedure of processing their film on site, scanning it and transmitting it via computer modems that operated at just a fraction of the speed that video footage or still photos can be transmitted today.

These days, photographers that are covering the World Series have the ability to simply remove memory cards from their cameras, view the photos on laptops and e-mail the digital images to their home offices. Larger news organizations typically assign runners to retrieve the cards from the photographers and bring them to workrooms located near the field under the stadium.

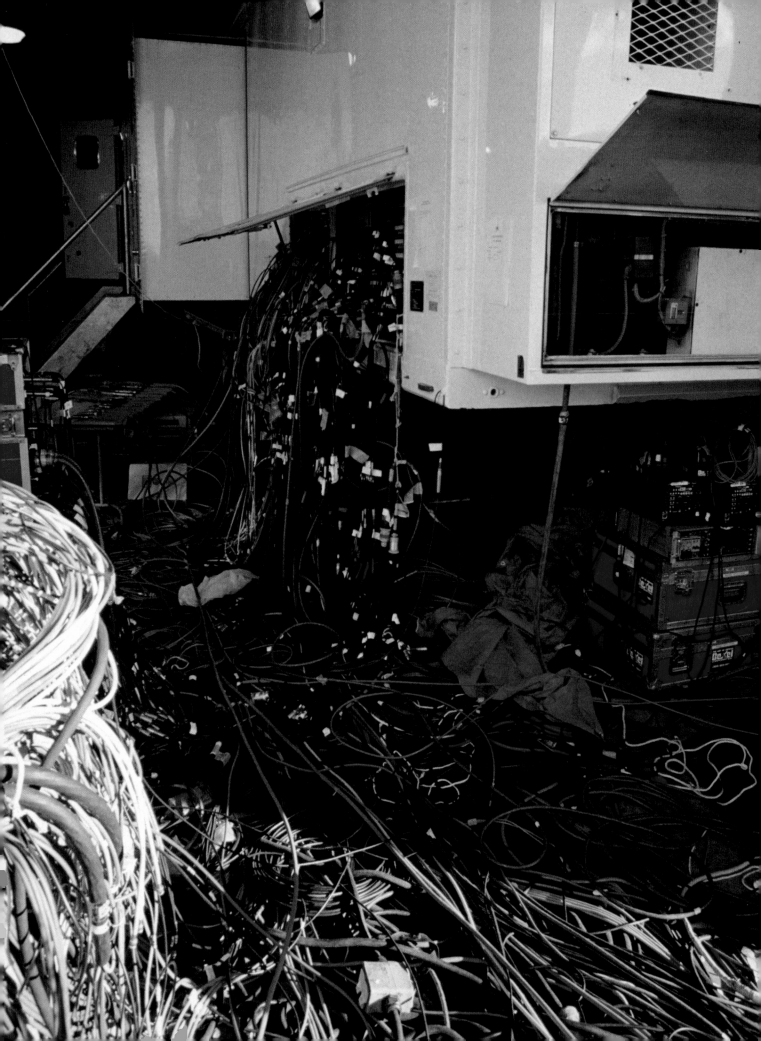

GAME 5: SHOWTIME

MORE THAN 44 MILLION PEOPLE WATCHED THE 1978 WORLD SERIES, FEATURING THE Los Angeles Dodgers against the New York Yankees in a rematch of the '77 Classic. And with just 337,304 ticketed fans in attendance at Dodger Stadium and Yankee Stadium during the six-game Series, the majority saw the Series on television rather than from the stands at the ballpark.

With so many epic moments in Fall Classic annals, few want to miss even a single inning of action. This means that fans around the world are increasingly likely to watch the contests on television or listen to them on the radio. In fact, some of the game's most poignant moments are remembered best through the words of broadcasters like Joe Buck and Vin Scully. Camera crews, broadcasters and producers work around the clock to seek out every interesting camera angle and uncover each unheard-of factoid to present the World Series in a fashion befitting its grandeur for those who can't make it to the ballpark.

BRINGING YOU THE BEST The NBC truck at the 1997 World Series.

STATE OF THE
ART A cameraman
prepares to shoot
Game 2 of the 2008
World Series.

PRIMETIME

WITH ITS CUTTING-EDGE GRAPHICS, BROADCAST INNOVATIONS and familiar on-air team of Joe Buck and Tim McCarver, Fox Sports has become virtually synonymous with the World Series. Not bad for a network that didn't even have a sports division until 1994, and didn't broadcast a baseball game of any sort until 1996.

World Series television broadcasts began in 1947 when NBC, CBS and the DuMont network shared coverage. The Series was shown in just four markets: New York City, Washington, D.C., Philadelphia and Schenectady, N.Y.

NBC presented the first coast-to-coast telecast of the World Series in 1951, with Jim Britt on play-by-play and Russ Hodges commentating. NBC held exclusive rights to the event through 1975, using broadcasters such as Vin Scully, Mel Allen and Curt Gowdy.

From 1976 to 1989, NBC and ABC alternated years of World Series coverage, with NBC handling even years and ABC odd. CBS began a four-year run in 1990, with Jack Buck and Sean McDonough each handling play-by-play duties for two years.

In 1995, the short-lived Baseball Network split coverage of the World Series between ABC and NBC. Fox Sports and NBC began to alternate years of Fall Classic coverage in 1996, with Fox taking even years and NBC taking odd.

In 2000, Fox signed a six-year agreement with MLB that included exclusive rights to the World Series through 2006, a deal later extended to include the Fall Classic through 2013.

Preparation for the World Series begins shortly after the All-Star Game, as producers begin compiling footage and background information on players from contending teams that might be participating in the Fall Classic. Any such stories must be somewhat generic since baseball players are a notoriously superstitious bunch and will not discuss anything postseason related — let alone the World Series — at that point.

Aside from rampant superstition, one of the biggest challenges in presenting the World Series is catering to both hardcore fans and also to those who might be tuning in for the very first time all year. Even the most avid baseball fan might not be that familiar with a team that surges unexpectedly to the top of the pack after a few seasons of anonymity.

"You spend a few innings of the first game sort of bringing people up to speed," said Pete Macheska, the lead producer for Fox's World Series coverage.

During the regular season, Fox usually uses seven or eight cameras for a Saturday broadcast. By 2008 the network was using

BEHIND THE MIC
Joe Buck (left) and McCarver call all the action for fans at home watching on TV.

30, including seven unmanned robotic cameras during the Fall Classic. That's twice as many total cameras as were used just a decade prior for the World Series. These days, a World Series broadcast on Fox involves an on-site crew of 125 individuals.

Some of the more unusual camera placements might include one high above center field that can provide a direct shot of home plate, unlike the standard manned camera that tends to be a little off on the ball-strike calls. There are also in-ground cameras in front of home plate and first base, and wireless cameras that allow a cameraman to walk onto the field after home runs and closely follow the batter from third base to home. Tampa Bay's Tropicana Field, one of the last remaining fixed-domed ballparks, provided Fox the opportunity to install cameras in the catwalks during the '08 Series.

With the many camera angles, umpires are scrutinized more than ever before. "Not that long ago, you might have seen two angles on a replay," Macheska said. "Now we can zoom in, do the super slo-mo and see it from every angle."

The technology can contribute to World Series plot lines, even inadvertently. In 2006, a television producer was monitoring Game 2 on a big-screen TV in a production truck and noticed what appeared to be a foreign substance on the pitching hand of the Tigers' Kenny Rogers. It was brought to the attention of Buck and McCarver during a commercial break and immediately discussed on air.

Thus began the pine tar controversy of that year's Fall Classic. The next day, when the Fox producers and on-air team were having their daily 15-minute sit-downs with each of the managers, Detroit's Jim Leyland expressed frustration and suggested the network went looking for controversy.

"The perception is that we go looking for that stuff and it's just not the case," Macheska said. "We follow and report on the story, we don't create it."

TECHNOLOGY

To watch a World Series broadcast from even the late 1990s on ESPN Classic or MLB licensed DVDs is startling given the many technological advances that have come about since, from super-slow motion replays to closer camera angles to the crisper images presented by HDTV.

It's often hard to imagine that simple graphics like the speed of the last pitch thrown and a constant scoreboard stripped across the top of the screen are actually relatively new innovations. By the end of 2013, 3-D broadcasts could even be commonplace.

Fox pioneered the more recent development of cutting frequently to the crowd and panning for fan reaction shots. The practice is something that previously occurred only following dramatic plays or to show notable celebrities who were in the house for that particular game. Now these types of shots are used strategically to build tension between pitches late in the game.

"The one thing that baseball has over other sports is this tension that can develop during a long at-bat," Pete Macheska said. "It could happen again and again and you're just hanging on every pitch. When that happens during the World Series, that's about as good as it gets if you're a baseball fan."

NYC CHAMPS A TV control room during the 1996 World Series at Yankee Stadium.

TRACKING With so many camera crews at the World Series, every bit of action — like Evan Longoria's foul catch here — is captured.

THROUGH THE WIRE
Bob Costas broadcasts for NBC
at Yankee Stadium during the
1999 World Series.

MLB PRODUCTIONS

DURING EVERY WORLD SERIES GAME SINCE THE LATE 1940S, MLB Productions has had its own crew on hand filming the event for the official World Series DVD and other MLB endeavors.

MLB Productions employs three cameras for each contest — one along each the first- and third-base lines and one roaming the stands. The first two cameras shoot high-definition footage at field level at the rate of 60 frames per second to create the dramatic, slow-motion feel that's a signature feature of the World Series DVD.

The TV broadcast usually places mics on two players or coaches during each World Series game, using just an occasional sound bite. But MLB Productions ends up with the entire audio file to use later.

MLB Productions also sends camera crews into the cities of the participating teams to capture the excitement of the area, often filming in bars, restaurants and other public gathering spots.

Because of Major League Baseball's complete access, crews have the ability to obtain footage that nobody else can. During the 2005 World Series, on the morning after Geoff Blum's 14th-inning homer to win Game 3, a team from MLB Productions documented a breakfast with Blum and his family. In 2008, they did a ride-along with James Shields of the Tampa Bay Rays on his way to the ballpark.

"It helps that we're not shooting live and players are comfortable with us because of our reputation," said Marc Caiafa, who spent 10 years as a producer with MLB Productions before taking a similar role with MLB Network. "We're MLB, after all. There's more of a comfort level with us."

In addition to the World Series DVD, other products that come from the Fall Classic include team highlight films. During the 2003 World Series, MLB produced a DVD commemorating the event's 100th anniversary. Since a package on "Great Japanese Players" was being created for MLB Network in 2008, it made sense to shoot extended footage of Akinori Iwamura of the Tampa Bay Rays.

World Series footage, like video from the regular season, goes into MLB's massive archives, along with news conferences held before and after games and on workout days during the Series. If a film producer or TV entity wishes to include actual baseball footage, they must license it from MLB.

MLB Productions interviews five to seven players per day during the World Series. A portion of what is captured won't be used in the official World Series DVD, but it will remain accessible to MLB Network.

"We'd rather film people on our own," Caiafa said. "But if there's a really good sound bite that comes out of a broadcast feed or press conference, we'll use it."

The World Series DVD typically runs between 1 hour and 75 minutes. In recent years, MLB also has produced boxed sets of entire Series. Top sellers include 1977 — the Yankees six-game defeat of the Dodgers featuring Reggie Jackson's three-homer game; 1978 — a repeat of the Yankees-Dodgers matchup; and 2004, when the Red Sox won their first title since 1918. With so much use for the footage, especially with the launch of MLB Network, it's no wonder MLB crews are busy during the event.

"You can never shoot too much," Caiafa said. "Eventually it will be used somewhere."

MR. OCTOBER Reggie Jackson's three-home run game in the 1977 World Series is hardly ever left out of a Fall Classic highlight collection.

RADIO

Baseball lends itself to radio better than any other sport, to the point that some of the more famous World Series calls have come from national radio broadcasts — even during the television era.

A year after his famous Kirk Gibson call in 1988, Jack Buck was teamed with Hall of Fame catcher Johnny Bench at San Francisco's Candlestick Park when an earthquake struck. After the quake hit, Buck said, "I must say about Johnny Bench, folks, if he moved that fast when he played, he would have never hit into a double play. I never saw anybody move that fast in my life."

The first World Series radio broadcast was in 1921 when sportswriter Grantland Rice provided telephone play-by-play over a special three-station hookup on KDKA (Pittsburgh), WJZ (Newark) and WBZ (East Springfield, Mass.). Rice wasn't at the game, but relayed reports that he received via telegraph wire.

During the 1922 World Series, play-by-play was broadcast directly from the site of the Fall Classic for the first time. Rice called the action, alongside Raymond Guy, an engineer at WJZ.

The radio broadcast remained popular even after NBC presented the first coast-to-coast television broadcast of the World Series in 1951. The World Series was broadcast on NBC Radio from 1957 to 1975 and on CBS Radio from 1976 to 1997. In 1998, the broadcast moved to ESPN Radio.

Longtime Phillies radio voice Harry Kalas got to make his first live call of a World Series win in 2008. When the Phillies last reached the Fall Classic in 1980 the national radio broadcast contracts prevented local broadcasters, like Kalas, from calling World Series games, a restriction lifted since the 1983 Fall Classic.

After waiting 28 seasons, Kalas got to take the microphone for the ninth inning and call the final out in 2008. Amid the celebration afterward, Kalas said he couldn't recall exactly what he said, stressing he had not scripted any of it. "As it happens it's spontaneous and I'm not sure how I called it, frankly," he said. "It has got to be spontaneous."

Just as players attempt to remain calm and treat a World Series game like any other, broadcasters try not to get carried away either.

"You call it as you would a game in the regular season but there's more excitement, more support," Kalas said. "You're going to be doing it in front of a sellout crowd, although [in 2008] we always did it in front of a sellout crowd, so it's just the top rung of the ladder when you're in the World Series. You're much more enthused, much more jacked-up all day long looking towards the game."

Broadcaster Dave Wills also got to call a World Series in 2008, in just his fourth year with the Tampa Bay Rays. But he admitted to giving some thought to a potential World Series winning call.

"You hear most announcers say they're just going to wait and see what comes to them, but even though you haven't written anything down, you've probably at least thought of something beforehand," Wills said. "It's an opportunity to make a call that could be out there forever."

GOOD OLD DAYS World Series
telegraphers set up at the Los Angeles
Railroad Station in 1926.

IN THE BOOTH

Six months before his 40th birthday, broadcaster Joe Buck quietly reached a television milestone, calling the entire Fall Classic for a record 11th time at the 2008 World Series. The mark was greater than that of legendary voices such as Mel Allen, Curt Gowdy and Vin Scully.

Teaming with Tim McCarver, Buck has become such a fixture in the booth that it's easy to forget that he did not make his World Series debut until 1996. Buck has handled play-by-play duties for the Series every year since 2000, along with 1996 and '98.

Buck has no trouble recalling his debut. Just 27 years old, he became the youngest man to call a national World Series broadcast since a 25-year-old Scully in 1953. Full of nervous energy before Game 1 between the Braves and Yankees in Yankee Stadium, Buck had to wait a day as the game was postponed by rain.

That Series, a wild six-game affair that featured the road team winning the first five games, ended when Yankees third baseman Charlie Hayes squeezed Mark Lemke's foul pop-up in the Bronx. Buck's clinching call was simple but perfect for the occasion: "The Yankees are world champions."

"After the fact I was glad something fell out of my mouth and I was able to put a stamp on the World Series because I was kind of ill-prepared for that moment," Buck said.

The 2001 World Series is also a memorable one for Buck, and not just because of the drama that was provided by the New York Yankees and Arizona Diamondbacks. With the entire country in mourning, just weeks removed from the 9/11 terrorist attacks, President George W. Bush threw out the first pitch at Yankee Stadium before Game 3.

"It was intense. And then you add the back-to-back nights of the late-inning home runs against Byung-Hyun Kim and Yankee Stadium was just literally shaking to its foundation. That's tough to top," he said.

Buck could not have been better prepared for his future in the booth, having spent his childhood around the St. Louis Cardinals and their longtime radio voice, his father, Jack Buck.

Jack called the 1990 and '91 World Series television broadcasts for CBS with McCarver, and handled the radio play-by-play of the Fall Classic for CBS Radio from 1983 to 1989.

During the 2002 World Series, Joe Buck paid tribute to his father, who had died four months earlier, by calling the final out of Game 6 with the phrase, "We'll see you tomorrow night." It was the same call Jack Buck made when Kirby Puckett's home run off Braves pitcher Charlie Leibrandt ended Game 6 of the 1991 World Series.

The younger Buck's call, "St. Louis has a World Series winner," at the end of the '06 World Series was a variation of his father's catchphrase at the end of Cardinals wins: "And that's a winner!"

Joe Buck says he's unlikely to produce a memorable line to match his father's radio call after Kirk Gibson's home run in Game 1 of the 1988 World Series: "I don't believe what I just saw."

"You can do a lot more with radio because you have to do the whole thing, not just laying back and letting the director cut pictures," he said. "You have to paint them with words. On TV, unless the crowd is dead, meaning the home team just got thumped by some play, it's much better to accent it and get out of the way and let the crowd go crazy. As a fan, I'd rather listen to that on TV. On radio, I want to hear the guy go nuts and say something I'll never forget."

Although Buck has also been Fox's lead NFL announcer, he says there's no comparing Super Bowl Sunday and the World Series.

"When an entire Series can come down to one pitch, one swing or one defensive play, those moments are rare in sports," he said. "Those are the moments you never forget, as a broadcaster and a fan, when you look at a battle like that. In my mind it doesn't get any better than that; no other sport provides that."

COMIC RELIEF

In recent years, Joe Buck has injected some subtle humor into the World Series broadcast, courtesy of late-night talk show host Conan O'Brien. During an appearance on *Late Night* prior to the 2006 Series, Buck was handed a gaudy necktie and agreed to wear it for Game 1.

Appearing on the show prior to the 2007 World Series, Buck mentioned that his friends challenge him to work certain phrases into the broadcast. O'Brien asked him to say "Jub-Jub" during the World Series and promised to donate $1,000 to charity if he did. During Game 1, Buck said, "Our own little Jub-Jub, Chris Myers, playing the role of weather person."

Buck was unable to deliver on O'Brien's challenge to work "buddy boy" into the 2008 All-Star Game broadcast, but he got it in during the World Series that year. During an on-camera shot, he turned to McCarver and said, "Well buddy-boy, it looks like we have a good game here tonight."

Buck says he tries to fulfill the requests since O'Brien will air them on his show, thus further promoting the World Series broadcast.

"In this day and age, you have to try and cross-promote whenever possible," he said. "To do it on a late-night show with a guy who is young and hip can be a good thing, so long as it fits with the broadcast."

NEW LEGEND
Broadcaster Joe Buck has
become a staple in the
booth at the Fall Classic.

FREE TACOS GALORE Ellsbury signs autographs and grabs his free taco for a World Series promotion in 2007.

PARTNERS

When Boston Red Sox outfielder Jacoby Ellsbury stole second base in the fourth inning of Game 2 of the 2007 World Series, he won a taco for every baseball fan in America as part of a Major League Baseball sponsorship deal with Taco Bell. The unique promotion was part of an ongoing effort by Major League Baseball to incorporate fans into the on-field action of the game, especially during the sport's biggest signature events — the All-Star Game and the World Series.

Starting in 2005, Pepsi, Major League Baseball's official soft drink since the mid-1990s, teamed up with the Walgreens drug-store chain for a contest offering a trip for four to the World Series, allowing one member of the winning party the thrill of a lifetime — to throw out a first pitch.

Similarly, Bank of America, another longtime partner of Major League Baseball, has offered fans the chance to work their way into the action before World Series games through its Extra Bases reward program. Created in 2006, the program has given fans with Bank of America Extra Bases credit cards the chance to redeem points for various baseball-themed prizes, including the opportunity to throw out a first pitch during the Fall Classic. Both the Pepsi/Walgreens and Bank of America first pitches are made prior to the traditional ceremonial first toss, which is thrown by a celebrity or dignitary.

Another way that Major League Baseball has given fans an opportunity to closely interact with the game was through a 2008 promotion with national partner Gillette, in which 48 would-be reporters competed for a chance to become the "Gillette Rookie Reporter." Clay Duerson, a Chicago Cubs fan, won the contest and earned the opportunity to report on Game 2 of the World Series from Tampa Bay.

"Our job is to extend the MLB experience and complement the amazing activities on the field," said John Brody, senior vice president of sales and marketing for Major League Baseball Properties. "Our sponsors enable fans to get closer to the sport through these special access opportunities."

Sponsorships play a key role in other aspects of the World Series beyond allowing fans to get closer to the game. Chevrolet has sponsored the Roberto Clemente Award and Most Valuable Player Award — the Phillies' right-handed stud, Cole Hamels, took home a red 2010 Camaro for his efforts in the 2008 Fall Classic — and Sharp Electronics has sponsored the Hank Aaron Award, which is presented prior to Game 4 of each World Series.

Unlike the Super Bowl, where the NFL replaces much of the sponsor signage in the host stadium with those of national sponsors, the signage at the two World Series sites stays pretty much the same as it is during the regular season. An exception took place in 2008, when ads for MLB Network — which launched in 2009 — were posted on the outfield walls in Philadelphia and Tampa Bay.

The rotating virtual signage behind home plate that's used to promote team sponsors during the regular season is used during the World Series for MLB sponsors or to promote upcoming programming on network television.

In the case of Taco Bell, fans were able to receive a free taco during a four-hour afternoon period several days after the stolen base. During the 2008 World Series, Rays shortstop Jason Bartlett swiped second base. That steal in the fifth inning of Game 1 not only gave America a chance to eat free tacos for the second time in two years, but it was an added bonus for Rays fans. Prior to that, all season long and into the playoffs, Tampa fans had enjoyed a promotion of free donuts from Dunkin' Donuts following a Rays win. Although Tampa Bay fell short of the world title, such promotions certainly get the fans involved in the game.

"These are the sort of things our partners bring that really reward the fans and accentuate the message around the game," Brody said. "Even casual fans can appreciate a free taco."

SUPPLY AND DEMAND Players like
Japan-native Akinori Iwamura necessitate
World Series broadcasts to other countries.

AROUND THE GLOBE

WHILE BASEBALL FANS IN THE UNITED STATES HAVE WATCHED THE MAJOR U.S. TV networks deliver the World Series broadcast, the rest of the world has gotten a much different perspective. Broadcasters from countries including the Dominican Republic, Japan, Mexico, Panama, Singapore and Venezuela set up their own announcing booths at each ballpark during the Fall Classic, while international branches of networks call the action live. Countries that don't send their own crew receive a special MLB International broadcast featuring play-by-play men and analysts that have included Ken Singleton, Gary Thorne, Joe Morgan, Rick Sutcliffe and Dave O'Brien. The MLBI broadcast team mixes audio with field-level sounds and its own commentary.

The countries with crews on site work hand-in-hand with the MLBI broadcast. If a producer informs broadcasters of an upcoming graphic about to appear on screen, the other broadcast teams will hear and be prepared to discuss it.

Many countries air the MLBI broadcast, and it reaches about 1 million U.S. and Canadian Armed Forces personnel through the Armed Forces Network. In some countries, broadcasters get the live feed and provide instant dubbed translation. The MLB International broadcast reaches 229 countries and is produced in about 13 languages each year.

One big misconception about the international feed, according to MLB International Vice President and Executive Producer Russell Gabay, is that the world is seeing the domestic TV broadcast with an additional camera and different announcers. In fact, Americans living overseas are often surprised to see the difference in the international broadcast. A customized first segment is produced for the foreign broadcasters on site, focusing on any international players of interest. MLB International runs its own graphics, in English, but both teams' lineups incorporate country-of-origin flags. When each team takes the field, the players appear on screen and announce their home countries, not unlike the way NFL players provide their college alma maters prior to games.

Since the level of baseball exposure varies among viewers around the world, analysts explain vernacular such as the double-switch or 6-4-3 double play. They even answer questions that viewers submit via e-mail. The e-mails illustrate the range of baseball knowledge around the world. A fan might, for example, ask for a broadcaster's thoughts on whether he would take the pitcher out if he were managing, or ask if a player can re-enter the game once he is pulled.

"The challenge is to take time to explain things, but not to the point where the avid fan gets annoyed," Gabay said.

Just as the national broadcast uses the virtual signage on the backstop to promote MLB sponsors and other network programming, the international feed employs the same technology to promote sponsors that have paid for country-specific advertising in Canada, Japan, Mexico and other parts of Latin America. Gabay's team creates special packages for use during country-specific broadcasts. During the 2008 World Series, the Dominican Republic broadcasters had heavy demand for replays of Domincan-born Carlos Pena's at-bats and other plays, even though the Rays first baseman struggled for much of the Series.

With Daisuke Matsuzaka, Hideki Okajima and Akinori Iwamura playing key roles in recent Fall Classics — Matsuzaka and Okajima for Boston in 2007 and Iwamura for Tampa Bay in '08 — there's been strong demand from the Japanese broadcasters on site for anything related to their countrymen.

Anyone still skeptical about the global growth of baseball need only step into the MLB International control truck during the World Series and hear the cacophony of foreign tongues delivering the broadcast.

"The differences can be a little startling at first," Gabay said. "But even people who just visit the truck during the World Series find that it's really pretty cool."

GAME 6:
THE MAKING OF
MEMORIES

A trip to the Fall Classic is a once in a lifetime experience, and everyone wants a souvenir to commemorate the event. For fans, the keepsakes include programs, hats, T-shirts or even a piece of game-used memorabilia. In the frenzy of crowning a new world champion, however, some merchandise isn't quite what it seems. That's why MLB authenticators employ a specially developed system to ensure the legitimacy of all items from the event. This secure system also ensures the viability of the artifacts heading to the Hall of Fame for display.

For players, simply playing the game they love can be reward enough. But mementos of the season can also come in the form of hardware handed out during the postseason. The Roberto Clemente and Hank Aaron Awards are two such honors. One thing that fans and ballplayers have in common during the Fall Classic is that no one wants to go home empty handed.

GET 'EM WHILE THEY'RE HOT A vendor at Fenway Park sells official programs prior to Game 2 of the 2007 World Series.

OFFICIAL WORLD SERIES SOUVENIRS

DURING THE WORLD SERIES, THERE'S NO SHORTAGE OF OFFICIAL merchandise available. From T-shirts to pennants and shot glasses, the types of souvenirs run the gamut. But the seemingly endless supply is often accompanied by counterfeit items, goods from vendors who hawk merchandise violating the trademarks of MLB and its players.

There are five ways to tell if an item purchased at the Fall Classic is officially licensed. First it must have an authorized hologram. A brand new type of hologram featuring a raised red stitch was introduced during the World Series in 2008. The raised stitch creates a sensory element, enhancing the hologram's effectiveness.

MLB's official silhouetted batter logo appears on all its products, along with identification of the MLB licensee that manufactures them. Trademark notices and clothing labels must be intact. A cut label means the item was misprinted or otherwise irregular and not intended for sale.

MLB takes an aggressive stance against vendors selling merchandise that is not officially licensed, working with local and national law officials to confiscate knock-off items and cease their distribution. During a World Series, MLB and law enforcement seize thousands of bootleg caps, shirts and other items from dozens of vendors. The goal is to remove the fakes from the market and pursue those who manufacture and distribute them.

"We do what we can to protect the consumer," said Ethan Orlinsky, general counsel for MLB Properties, baseball's licensing arm. "We take pride in the quality of items produced and don't want our fans getting burned by paying for goods that don't live up to the high standards they rightfully expect of our licensed products."

The sale of counterfeit and unlicensed merchandise also impacts host cities since merchants without sales permits likely aren't charging sales tax or reporting their earnings.

Because of the low cost of screen printing and other new technologies, counterfeiting has never been easier. So, MLB goes to great lengths to protect its consumers.

In 2008, unlicensed entrepreneurs made "Rayhawk" T-shirts, inspired by the haircut adopted by Rays players. Additionally, shirts and other paraphernalia were available proclaiming the Rays "Beasts of the East."

According to Orlinsky, the sale of T-shirts, hats or any other merchandise featuring team names, logos, slogans or other indicia violate the league's or teams' trademark rights if the product manufacturer does not have permission to use such indicia from MLB Properties.

"The counterfeiters are trading off the goodwill of the brand owners," Orlinsky said. "Sometimes we'll send cease-and-desist letters, but other times we have no choice but to sue."

During the World Series, Major League Baseball Properties has as many as 50 employees on site investigating counterfeit and unlicensed products.

"We don't just stop at the ballpark," Orlinsky said. "We do what we can to stop the illegal activity at its source. The shirts we seize from someone selling on the street is often our link to finding the manufacturing facility."

SUBWAY SERIES A
Dodgers vendor sells official
merchandise at the 1952
World Series.

SEEING RED Cardinals fans buy official
merchandise at Busch Stadium before Game 4
of the 2004 World Series in St. Louis.

AUTHENTICATED MERCHANDISE

NOT LONG AFTER THE PHILADELPHIA PHILLIES CLINCHED the 2008 World Series, Michael Posner walked off the field at Citizens Bank Park carrying something that most Philadelphians there that night would have given an eye for — home plate.

But Posner is not a bold Phillies fan or an ambitious memorabilia collector. He's the authentication manager for Major League Baseball, in charge of overseeing the operations of a program that catalogs and authenticates virtually everything that is associated with a particular Fall Classic game.

The program began in 2001 in response to an FBI investigation dubbed "Operation Bullpen" that confirmed what many baseball authorities, and even fans, had long suspected: The unregulated sports memorabilia industry was full of scam artists hawking forged autographs and bogus collectibles.

MLB assembled a team of about 125 authenticators to certify every item taken from games during the regular season and the playoffs. By placing a tamper-proof hologram on the product and immediately scanning it into a database accessible through MLB.com, they ensure that collectors purchasing any item marketed as game-used can have piece of mind, not to mention a very cool souvenir.

When players return to the clubhouse after a game, they have to share space with authenticators who are already hard at work in the room with sheets of holograms and scanners. Nothing is off limits, not even jock straps.

"It gets kind of crazy sometimes," said Howard Shelton, another of MLB's authentication account managers. "I generally wear gloves."

During any World Series, thousands of products are authenticated, from home plate itself to the balls and bats used to the champagne bottles (and of course the corks) that are part of Fall Classic-clinching celebrations.

The players even get their own collectibles authenticated, which on the surface seems odd if they have no intention of ever parting with them. "This way they're protected in case somebody goes on eBay claiming to sell something the player used in the World Series," Posner said. "Only the player, or whoever they give the item to, has the authenticated item."

Although some of the authenticated merchandise is sold on MLB.com, many items never reach the sports memorabilia marketplace. Teams donate some collectibles to charitable auctions and other times they will distribute the items to sponsors and front-office staff members.

During the World Series, authenticators position themselves near the dugouts, usually in the camera wells, to authenticate items as soon as they are removed from the game. A new set of bases is brought out every three innings, and the game-used ones are immediately authenticated.

In addition to placing a hologram on the product and scanning it into MLB's database, the authenticator will also include a detailed description of the item. Whenever players sign boxes of baseballs during the World Series, an authenticator is on hand. Some of the more unusual Fall Classic products that get authenticated include the team-logo plastic draped over the winning club's lockers during championship celebrations, vials of dirt from the infield, and the locker nameplates created especially for the postseason.

Even seemingly trivial items such as rosin bags and lineup cards get authenticated during the World Series. About the only thing ineligible for authentication is a home run ball thrown back onto the field by a fan.

"Who's to say the fan threw back the same ball?" Posner said. "Chances are it's the same one, but we won't authenticate something unless we have witnessed it and are positive."

That might seem unnecessarily strict, but Major League Baseball's system is widely hailed as tamper-proof in the memorabilia industry and its authenticators, who work every regular-season game, are all involved with law enforcement.

"We're suited for this since we're used to handling evidence and dealing with chain of custody," said Joe Jesiolkiewic, a former St. Petersburg, Fla., police officer who now serves as an MLB authenticator in the Tampa Bay area.

"If we're there to witness it, we'll authenticate it," Posner said. "By creating a process where an item can't be disputed, we're helping to record the history of the game."

During the World Series, authenticators position themselves near the dugouts, usually in the camera wells, to authenticate items as soon as they are removed from the game. A new set of bases is brought out every three innings, and the game-used ones are immediately authenticated.

THE REAL DEAL
Game-used baseballs are
authenticated alongside
the field during Game 1
of the 2008 World Series.

METS MEMENTOS
Fans storm the field at
Shea Stadium after the
1969 Mets clinch the
World Series with a win
over the Orioles.

WORLD SERIES MEMORABILIA

GIVEN THE POPULARITY OF THE WORLD SERIES, IT'S NOT SURPRISING THAT EACH YEAR memorabilia from the Fall Classic becomes highly sought after. While many fans tend to save relatively inexpensive and easily obtainable products like programs, game tickets, pennants and other knick-knacks, serious collectors mostly desire items that were either used in the game or awarded to a player for his performance.

Robert Edward Auctions, a prominent baseball memorabilia auction house in Watchung, N.J., sells many World Series-related items in a large annual auction. Some high-profile sales include a bat used by Joe DiMaggio in the 1947 World Series ($23,200), a home jersey worn by Mariano Rivera in the 1998 Series ($10,575), Dwight Gooden's personal 1986 World Series trophy ($13,920) and a bat used by Bobby Thomson during the 1951 Fall Classic ($11,500).

New York Yankees memorabilia is the most popular among collectors, especially if it's related to storied clubs such as the 1927 or '61 teams. Items from famous — or infamous — teams such as the 1969 New York Mets and the 1919 Chicago White Sox are also popular.

A World Series ring, MVP Award or personal trophy will sometimes appear in an auction. Although some come from players who either no longer want them or have fallen on tough times financially, other rings come from front office staff members. Occasionally, a player's estate sells the memorabilia since its value outweighs any sentimental attachment. In 2008, Thurman Munson's widow, Diana, placed a number of the late Yankees catcher's World Series items in an auction held during All-Star break festivities in New York.

A full-sized replica of the 1978 World Series trophy, made for the Yankees captain, sold for $207,000 during a sale conducted by Hunt Auctions at Major League Baseball's 2008 DHL All-Star FanFest auction in Manhattan. Munson's 1977 World Series ring sold for $143,750 and his ring from the 1978 World Series for $97,750.

Perhaps the most famous sale of World Series memorabilia took place in 1992, when actor and noted baseball fan Charlie Sheen paid $93,500 for the ball that the Mets' Mookie Wilson hit through Bill Buckner's legs during Game 6 of the 1986 World Series.

After Ray Knight scored the winning run on Wilson's dribbler down the first-base line, the ball was retrieved by right-field umpire Ed Montague and given to Arthur Richman, the Mets' traveling secretary, who six years later consigned it to Leland's Auctions.

Wilson signed the ball: "To Arthur: The ball won it for us. Mookie Wilson. 10-25-86."

When Sheen sold much of his baseball memorabilia collection in 2000, the buyer of the "Buckner Ball" was songwriter Seth Swirsky, who has perhaps the most impressive collection of noteworthy World Series items.

Swirsky's collection also includes the third home run ball that Reggie Jackson hit in Game 6 of the 1977 World Series that helped clinch the world title for the Yankees, the last balls used in the 1945 and 1981 World Series, and the only known bottle of champagne from the aborted Red Sox celebration in 1986. The unopened bottle of "Cranberry Blush," produced by the Commonwealth Winery, reads "Boston Red Sox 1986 Champions."

The unused bottle of bubbly illustrates how the most desirable World Series memorabilia is connected to baseball's most storied franchises — especially when the particular World Series or overall season was particularly memorable — even if the team didn't win.

"Certain teams have this magical appeal to collectors," said Rob Lifson, president of Robert Edward Auctions. "If they cap off a terrific season with a dramatic win in the World Series, that's going to produce some popular memorabilia."

**HUNTINGTON
AVENUE**
AMERICAN LEAGUE
BASE BALL
GROUNDS

Autumn Glory
A POSTSEASON CELEBRATION

Who is the Best? For a hundred years, baseball's top clubs have answered that question in the game's greatest pressure cooker—the modern World Series. The events of the Series have become legend, and its stars have made an impact on American culture far beyond the playing field. The Fall Classic magnifies both victory and defeat. Teams, players and fans are never so joyful, or so heartbroken, as during these championship games.

Don Larsen, Bill Mazeroski, Carlton Fisk and Reggie Jackson are just a few of the players who are known, even by non-fans, for their Series heroics. Although expansion, division play and wild cards have modified the postseason landscape, winning the World Series remains baseball's ultimate dream.

HALL OF FAME

EACH YEAR, THE WORLD SERIES FEATURES PLAYERS WHO MIGHT ONE day, years in the future, be honored with induction into the National Baseball Hall of Fame and Museum in Cooperstown, N.Y.

But each time a new world champion is crowned, artifacts from the Fall Classic arrive within days to be displayed as part of the *Autumn Glory* exhibit, which features such historic items as the final-out ball from the 1903 World Series, the mitt that Yogi Berra wore to catch Don Larsen's perfect game in 1956, and the bat (which is now bronzed) that Bill Mazeroski used to hit the dramatic World Series-winning home run in 1960.

Much of the *Autumn Glory* exhibit is permanent, but one display case is dedicated to the most recent World Series. By mid-November, items from that year's World Series are on display, and artifacts from the previous Fall Classic are stored for future use.

Public relations officials from the Hall of Fame staff work during each Fall Classic to acquire donations from players and teams that best represent the event. During the World Series, the Hall officials on site keep in contact with curators in Cooperstown to determine which artifacts would best tell the story of that particular World Series.

"The players are incredibly generous, and we understand if they want to keep a particular item," said Craig Muder, director of communications for the Hall of Fame. "But usually they're receptive to the idea."

Long before the ownership dispute between Doug Mientkiewicz and the Boston Red Sox over the final-out ball from the historic 2004 World Series, it was customary for players who recorded the last out — often first basemen or catchers — to retain possession of the balls. Many of those, including Mientkiewicz's, end up in Cooperstown.

The Hall of Fame receives all different types of artifacts at the conclusion of the World Series, from bats — like the one that Philadelphia hurler Joe Blanton used to belt the first World Series home run by a pitcher in 34 years in 2008 — to balls, press pins, programs, photographs, spikes and helmets.

Such artifacts add to the Hall's legendary collection of World Series memorabilia that dates back to 1903, the year considered to be the start of the modern Fall Classic. But the Hall's treasure trove includes items from every era, for example a bat used by outfielder Earle Combs in 1927 — when he was a member of the Yankees' Murderers' Row team, widely considered the greatest team ever to come together. That year, Combs scored six runs against the Pittsburgh Pirates in New York's sweep of the World Series. Also on display in the Hall is the final-out ball from Game 1, which was donated by Yankees legend Lou Gehrig and his wife, before he passed away.

The Hall of Fame's World Series collection includes the catcher's mask worn by Mickey Owen during Game 4 of the 1941 World Series for the Brooklyn Dodgers, a game that the New York Yankees won, decided

WALLS OF HISTORY
Entrance to the World Series *Autumn Glory* exhibit in Cooperstown.

BEHIND THE GLASS Artifacts on display in the *Autumn Glory* exhibit at the Hall of Fame.

on Owens' costly passed ball, before the Bombers went on to take the Series in Game 5. A jersey worn by left-handed hurler Jerry Koosman for the 1969 Miracle Mets is on display. Koosman pitched his team to a first-place season with a 100-62 record, and a World Series championship.

A ball from the first World Series night game, Game 4 of the 1971 Fall Classic, can be found in the Hall. That famous game matched the Pirates against the Baltimore Orioles, and took place at Three Rivers Stadium in Pittsburgh. The Pirates are also represented by reliever Kent Tekulve's gold star-covered cap from 1979.

MEMORY LANE Hall of Famer Sparky Anderson views artifacts from Detroit's 1984 World Series win at the Hall of Fame in Cooperstown, N.Y.

Although the National Baseball Hall of Fame has a collection of priceless pieces that are always available for the public to enjoy, the World Series additions are a hugely popular attraction in Cooperstown when they're unveiled each November, upon the conclusion of the baseball postseason.

"Fans are able to see these important artifacts from just days ago from an event they witnessed, at least on television," said Tom Shieber, the senior curator for the Hall of Fame. "Right away they can view them within the context of so many great moments in World Series history."

HALL OF FAME GOLDMINE

Already with thousands upon thousands of artifacts at its disposal, the National Baseball Hall of Fame and Museum won't see its vault empty any time soon. Every season, the Hall receives myriad items from big events and milestones, such as Ichiro Suzuki's game-used spikes from the day he rapped his 3,000th professional hit. Of course, no event has more sought-after items than the World Series, and the Hall of Fame makes sure to collect plenty. Just take a look at the following sampling, which offers a taste of just a few World Series artifacts put on display by the Museum:

• The ball thrown by Boston pitcher Bill Dinneen to strike out Honus Wagner and end the first ever World Series in 1903.

• The trophy given to Manager John McGraw by his New York Giants players after winning the 1921 World Series.

• The glove worn by Willie Mays in Game 1 of the 1954 Series. Mays' running, over-the-shoulder catch in that game has become an enduring Fall Classic moment.

• The glove worn by Tommie Agee of the Miracle Mets during Game 3 of the 1969 Series. That game served as a turning point in the Mets' eventual victory over Baltimore.

• The spikes worn by St. Louis Cardinals' speedy shortstop Ozzie Smith during the 1982 Fall Classic, in which St. Louis beat the Milwaukee Brewers in seven games.

• The jersey worn by New York Yankees star rookie shortstop Derek Jeter during the 1996 Series, in which his team took down the Atlanta Braves.

• The bloody sock worn by Curt Schilling during a post-surgery, Game 2 pitching performance in 2004 — the year Boston won its first title since 1918.

• Fall Classic MVP Cole Hamels' home jersey from the Series-clinching Game 5 in 2008. Hamels gave up just four runs in 13 innings during the Series.

PRESS PINS

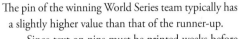

THE PHILADELPHIA A'S WERE THE FIRST TO ISSUE pins to members of the media covering the World Series. The original models were more like medallions, but by 1916 clubs had evolved a pin-back version. The pins originally served as press credentials, with reporters wearing them on their lapels. Once teams began to issue laminated passes, the pins served as keepsakes for those covering the event. The team-logo pins aren't available to the public, and have become sought-after collectibles.

Like most sports memorabilia, press pins were not viewed as collectibles when they were first used. Since very few were saved — and relatively few issued — early press pins now can sell for thousands of dollars at memorabilia auctions.

The pin of the winning World Series team typically has a slightly higher value than that of the runner-up.

Since text on pins must be printed weeks before the playoffs, some teams create pins but never reach the playoffs. These "phantom" pins are sometimes sold or given to fans and are often rarer than those of the teams that participate in the Fall Classic.

Like most baseball collectibles, an item's popularity has much to do with the teams involved. Press pins for the Chicago Cubs are treasured, as well as those of the 1955 world champion Brooklyn Dodgers. Even though the New York Yankees have produced the most press pins over the years, the franchise's popularity still makes those pins highly sought-after, especially the vintage ones.

HANK AARON AWARD

THE HANK AARON AWARD IS PRESENTED PRIOR TO GAME 4 of each World Series to the best offensive performer in both the AL and NL. Created in 1999 to honor the 25th anniversary of Aaron breaking Babe Ruth's all-time home run record, it was the first major baseball award introduced in more than 25 years.

Initially, a scoring system was used to select the winner. Hits, home runs and RBI were assigned point values and the winner was the player with the most total points during the year. In 2000, MLB implemented a ballot system whereby each club's radio and TV play-by-play men and color analysts were given three votes for each league. Beginning in 2003, fans were also given the opportunity to vote through MLB.com. Fan votes account for 30 percent of the points, with the votes of broadcasters and analysts accounting for the remaining 70 percent.

In its first decade, Alex Rodriguez won the award four times. Only twice has a player participating in the World Series received the Hank Aaron Award — Barry Bonds in '02 and Manny Ramirez in '04.

Players consider the award a prestigious honor, especially since Aaron travels to the World Series to present it alongside Commissioner Bud Selig. Starting in 2007, Sharp Electronics Corporation served as the award's presenting sponsor.

"To win this award, I'm a little humbled by it," said 2008 winner Kevin Youkilis after a fine season with the Red Sox. "It's an honor just to be named in the same sentence with somebody that exemplified so much in this game."

ROBERTO CLEMENTE AWARD

ONE OF BASEBALL'S MOST PRESTIGIOUS AWARDS ISN'T JUST A recognition of on-field performance, statistics or win-loss records. The Roberto Clemente Award, presented by Chevrolet, is awarded prior to Game 3 at each World Series. It is given to the player who demonstrates the values that Clemente displayed in his commitment to helping others, in addition to his greatness on the field.

When the award was first bestowed by MLB in 1971, it was called the Commissioner's Award, but it was renamed in Clemente's honor in 1973 after the Pittsburgh Pirates outfielder died tragically in a plane crash while traveling to provide relief to earthquake victims in Nicaragua.

"As a national pastime and as a social institution, we in baseball have important social responsibilities that we gladly welcome," Commissioner Bud Selig said in 2008, while presenting the award to St. Louis's Albert Pujols. "Roberto Clemente is the symbol of our social awareness and our effort to give back to all the communities in which we play the game."

Each club nominates one of its own players for the award in September, and the winner is then selected from those 30 nominees. The past winners of the award represent some of baseball's most prominent names from the last four decades. The list is made up of several Hall of Famers and other well-respected contributors including Dale Murphy, Brooks Robinson, Lou Brock, Rod Carew, Gary Carter, John Smoltz, Al Kaline, Willie Mays, Phil Niekro, Kirby Puckett, Cal Ripken Jr., Don Baylor, Ozzie Smith, Willie Stargell and Dave Winfield.

In 2001, Curt Schilling was helping the Arizona Diamondbacks to a World Series championship when he received the award. It was especially meaningful since he grew up a Pirates fan and the first game he attended in person was Clemente's last.

BEST MAN Bob DuPuy (left), MLB's president and COO, and Clemente's sons present Smoltz (second from left) with the Clemente Award in 2005.

Several years before receiving the honor, Schilling vowed to use his platform as a Big Leaguer for something that would warrant consideration for the award. He eventually launched a foundation dedicated to curing ALS (Lou Gehrig's Disease).

"I looked at my wife when they were handing out the Clemente Award at the World Series in 1993, and I said to her, 'If I play long enough and I stay healthy enough, that's the one award I want to win before I'm done playing,'" Schilling said. "Because to win that award, it will not matter how many wins or strikeouts I have; I will have made a difference in peoples' lives."

Every year, Chevrolet donates to the winner's charity as well as to the Roberto Clemente Sports City in Puerto Rico — an organization that gives kids access to recreational sports facilities.

In 2006, Carlos Delgado received the Clemente Award for work with his foundation, Extra Bases, which assists underprivileged kids. Among other initiatives, the foundation puts together an annual pre-Thanksgiving feast for hundreds of homeless, underprivileged and handicapped children in Delgado's hometown of Aguadilla, Puerto Rico, where Delgado helps prepare and hand out the food. Like previous recipients of the award, Delgado was emotional upon receiving the honor from Selig and Vera Clemente, Roberto's widow. The award carried special meaning for Delgado, who chose to wear No. 21 with the New York Mets in honor of Clemente.

"It is an extreme honor for me to be selected for an award that bears the name of Roberto Clemente. He was a Hall of Fame player and a Hall of Fame person," Delgado said. "Roberto's legacy to me is that it's an athlete's obligation to give back. That's what I have tried to do throughout my career."

HELPING HANDS Vera Clemente helps present Delgado with the Roberto Clemente Award before Game 3 of the 2006 World Series.

THE RBI PROGRAM

AFTER THE NATIONAL ANTHEM AND SHORTLY BEFORE THE FIRST pitch of a World Series game, a group of young athletes takes the field for a special presentation. The kids, anywhere from 13 to 18 years old, represent the champions of the three divisions of the Reviving Baseball in Inner Cities (RBI) program, an MLB-owned initiative created in 1988 to increase inner city and urban youth interest and participation in baseball and softball.

Since its development by former Big Leaguer John Young, RBI has thrived thanks in particular to its first national presenting sponsor, MLB partner KPMG, one of the nation's Big Four accounting firms.

RBI has a presence in 206 communities in North America, Puerto Rico and the Caribbean. The program's alumni include more than 180 Major League draftees and Big Leaguers such as Carl Crawford and Coco Crisp.

During the World Series pregame ceremony, KPMG chairman Tim Flynn presents a $1 million check for the RBI program to Tim Brosnan, MLB's executive vice president of business.

KPMG made its first presentation before Game 3 of the 2007 World Series. The following year, the ceremony was held prior to Game 2 in St. Petersburg, Fla., an appropriate venue given the Rays' connections to RBI.

Tampa Bay's Crawford grew up in Houston and played in an RBI program there. He posed with the winners in '08: four each from the Junior Boys (13–15 year olds) from Detroit; the Senior Boys (16–18 year olds) from Los Angeles; and Girls Softball (15–18 year olds) from the Dominican Republic.

Crawford's experience supports the widespread view that the programs assist kids in staying busy, challenging their minds and bodies on the baseball field rather than leaving them idle. It also helped him gain exposure he might not have had otherwise.

"Options were limited for a guy like me," Crawford said. "RBI allowed me to be seen by a group of people who normally wouldn't have seen me."

Blue Jays pitcher Jesse Litsch also played RBI baseball. Growing up in St. Petersburg, Fla., Litsch's father, Rick, couldn't afford to pay the travel-team fees. So Jesse played RBI baseball in the shadow of Tropicana Field.

"College and pro scouts need to check out RBI," the righty said. "You can find a lot of diamonds in the rough."

Before Game 2 of the 2008 Series, Major League Baseball distributed a special 32-page program that chronicled the RBI initiative. Such efforts, along with footage of the pregame presentation shown later in the TV broadcast of Game 2, could introduce more children from underserved communities to RBI.

"That's the greater purpose we're trying to achieve," said David James, MLB's director of RBI. "If those images allow us to reach young [people] and get them involved with RBI, while allowing us to thank the people working with RBI leagues locally, and our national sponsor, then we are accomplishing our goals of providing more baseball and softball opportunities to underserved young men, young women and underserved communities."

GAME 7: THE GLORY

STARS ARE BORN AND LEGACIES ARE FORGED AFTER A TEAM RECORDS THE FINAL OUT of the World Series. They are world champions. But the journey for the players on the field and the staff behind the scenes is not over.

As the world championship gear is rushed out to those celebrating on the infield, manufacturers of that licensed merchandise immediately begin mass-production of shirts and hats. Clubhouse managers brace for the champagne celebration in the locker room, MLB officials prepare for the presentation of the Commissioner's Trophy, votes are cast for the World Series MVP, and memorabilia hounds size up potential keepsakes from the Series. There is a flurry of activity that must take place once the World Series winner is decided, executed by hard-working folks whose jobs continue even after that final out is recorded.

ON TOP OF THE WORLD The 1996 Yankees celebrate their first world title in 18 years.

CELEBRATION TIME
After winning a World
Series, players — like
Jimmy Rollins of the 2008
Phillies here — try on new
championship gear and
soak in the moment.

PARTY ATTIRE

WITHIN MOMENTS OF A WORLD SERIES-CLINCHING WIN, players and coaches from the victorious team don caps and T-shirts proclaiming them World Series champions.

Although the detail of the "world champions" gear — which arrives at the on-field celebration bearing the name and logo of the winning team — results in the assumption that it's freshly printed, it has actually been ready for weeks, and in some cases months. Since the World Series logo is designed about one year in advance, it's possible for official Major League Baseball licensees, like New Era and Majestic Athletic, to get a head start on designing the clubhouse celebration gear. This means they'll have plenty of product ready upon the culmination of the World Series.

New Era has designed the World Series champions hat in a way that everything can be stitched and printed in advance with the exception of a specific team logo disc that appears in the front of the hat. When teams begin clinching playoff spots in mid-September, hundreds of thousands of discs are printed for each team still in contention.

A small quantity of hats for each participating team is printed prior to the start of the Fall Classic and kept in storage at the ballparks, along with corresponding T-shirts. Once the World Series is clinched, mass production begins on the hats that will be available to the public.

Since T-shirts are much easier and quicker to produce than hats, Majestic Athletic has been able to print to order when it comes time to produce shirts for fans, as well as create a small quantity prior to the World Series for both participating teams. The T-shirts and hats are kept together and travel with the teams to the site of Games 3 through 5 and, if necessary, back to the site of Games 6 and 7.

Although the hats and shirts that proclaim the losing team "World Series champions" would undoubtedly become sought-after collectibles, they aren't distributed — at least not in North America. MLB, not wanting to waste several dozen T-shirts and hats, works with the charity WorldVision, who distributes the excess items to those in need in Third World countries. This also includes items produced for the two teams that end up losing the League Championship Series.

The World Series is a hectic time for the employees responsible for mass-producing the merchandise. They watch the event differently than most fans. If a team is on the verge of clinching, the staff must be prepared for an all-night printing of commemorative gear.

"They'll put out 90,000 hats as soon as possible, pull a double shift and take the next day off," said Howard Smith, MLB's senior vice president of licensing. "Then they'll come back and finish the rest that need to be made."

Many other MLB licensees also spring into action once the World Series ends, creating special products in every imaginable category. That's been a common occurrence in recent years with the 2004 Boston Red Sox, the 2005 Chicago White Sox and the 2008 Philadelphia Phillies winning the World Series.

"A white-hot market is created overnight," Smith said. "Everyone wants a piece of it, claiming that their team is finally a world champion."

DRESSED FOR SUCCESS Smith, MLB's senior vice president of licensing, distributes "world champions" gear to the Phillies on the field following their World Series victory in 2008.

DODGER BLUES Jackie
Robinson laments after the
Brooklyn Dodgers loss in Game
7 of the 1952 World Series to the
crosstown-rival New York Yankees.

LOSING CLUBHOUSE

A LOSING CLUBHOUSE CAN BE A SOMBER PLACE DURING THE REGULAR SEASON. BUT AFTER a World Series loss, the room is downright funereal. No music is played, and the volume is turned down on any televisions that are on. If a team is on the road when its season ends, clubhouse attendants are usually hustling to remove equipment bags in preparation for the team's flight home.

When the clubhouse opens to the media after a cooling-off period, it's common for the room to already be empty. Some players who did not play in the game will have quickly showered and departed, without comment. Others who did play might take long showers, needing additional time to overcome the initial shock of losing and compose themselves before addressing the media.

As is the case during the regular season, there are players who assume the unofficial role of team spokesmen, regardless of how, or even if, they played that night. Usually veteran position players shoulder much of the media burden, allowing younger teammates, especially young stars, to avoid it.

The media recognize such go-to guys, and often rely on them after a Series loss. After the clinching game of a World Series, however, most players make themselves available, not only understanding that it's the professional thing to do, but also that it's better to address the matter immediately than have to revisit the loss in interviews throughout the winter.

In 1988, Dennis Eckersley stood at his locker following Game 1 of the World Series, after giving up the famous limp-off home run to Kirk Gibson, addressing wave after wave of reporters asking the same questions. Throughout the Atlanta Braves' magical run of 14 division championships that produced just one World Series title, starters Tom Glavine and John Smoltz endured marathon post-game sessions whenever a Braves season fell short, including losses in the 1996 and '99 World Series.

Eventually reporters return to the press boxes or to the winning clubhouse, allowing players on the losing team to make their way out of the ballpark. If a team loses the World Series on the road, nameplates are removed from their locker stalls. If defeat comes at home, the players will return the following day to pack up their belongings for the offseason. In either case, it's a quiet reminder that the season ended just shy of the ultimate goal.

ANGUISH Padres pitcher Kevin Brown in the clubhouse after a World Series sweep by the Yankees in '98.

SPOILS OF SUCCESS World Series MVPs take home prizes like a trophy and this Chevy, won by Jermaine Dye of the White Sox in 2005.

WORLD SERIES MVP

As if becoming a World Series champion was not a sufficient reward, the Most Valuable Player has also received a trophy and a car from Chevrolet, which has served as the Official Vehicle of Major League Baseball since 2005, and previously from 1985 through 1996.

The World Series MVP Award was originally given out by the editors of *SPORT* magazine in 1955. These days, a committee of baseball writers and Major League Baseball officials decides on the tournament's Most Valuable Player.

Through 2008, pitchers had won the World Series MVP Award 26 times, including 12 of the first 14 years it was given out. Numerous Hall of Famers have won the award, including two-time honorees Sandy Koufax (1963 and '65 with the Los Angeles Dodgers), Bob Gibson (1964 and '67 with the St. Louis Cardinals) and Reggie Jackson. Known as "Mr. October" for his clutch hitting in the World Series, Jackson is the only player to win the award for two teams, the 1973 Oakland Athletics and the 1977 New York Yankees.

Some of the more unlikely Most Valuable Players of World Series past include Donn Clendenon of the 1969 New York Mets (.357, three home runs, four RBI), Bucky Dent of the 1978 New York Yankees (.417, three runs, seven RBI) and David Eckstein of the 2006 St. Louis Cardinals (.364, three runs, four RBI). A good number of light-hitting catchers have boosted their offensive production during the World Series and taken home MVP honors. It's a group that includes the Los Angeles Dodgers backstop Steve Yeager (.286, two home runs, four RBI), who shared the award with his teammates Pedro Guerrero and Ron Cey in 1981, Baltimore's Rick Dempsey in 1983 (.385, one home run, two RBI) and Toronto's Pat Borders in 1992 (.450, one home run, three RBI).

But some ballplayers have been able to carry their regular-season dominance into the World Series. Players who have won a league MVP Award in the same season as the World Series MVP include Koufax, Baltimore's Frank Robinson, Jackson, Pittsburgh's Willie Stargell (who shared his regular-season National League MVP honor with St. Louis's Keith Hernandez in 1979) and Philadelphia's Mike Schmidt.

Pitchers who have won a Cy Young Award in the same season as the World Series Most Valuable Player include Bob Turley of the 1958 Yankees, Whitey Ford of the 1961 Yankees, Koufax in both 1963 and '65, Bret Saberhagen of the 1985 Kansas City Royals, Orel Hershiser of the 1988 Dodgers and Randy Johnson, who shared his 2001 World Series MVP Award with mound-mate Curt Schilling, when their Arizona Diamondbacks emerged victorious over the Yankees in seven emotionally charged games weeks after the 9/11 terrorist attacks.

ULTIMATE MVPs

If the ultimate goal for a team is to win the World Series, and the ultimate goal of every player is to help his team win, then only a handful of players since the World Series MVP Award was implemented in 1955 have been perfect MVPs. Listed below are the five men who were named both league MVP and World Series MVP in the same season, as well as their regular-season and World Series stats.

	IP	W-L	ERA	K	BB
Sandy Koufax, 1963					
Regular Season	311	25-5	1.88	306	58
World Series	18	2-0	1.50	23	3

	AVG	OBP	HR	RBI	SLG
Frank Robinson, 1966					
Regular Season	.316	.410	49	122	.637
World Series	.286	.375	2	3	.857
Reggie Jackson, 1973					
Regular Season	.293	.383	32	117	.531
World Series	.310	.355	1	6	.586
Willie Stargell, 1979					
Regular Season	.281	.352	32	82	.552
World Series	.400	.375	3	7	.833
Mike Schmidt, 1980					
Regular Season	.286	.380	48	121	.624
World Series	.381	.462	2	7	.714

Schmidt, 1980

A handful of players who dominated for the duration of the postseason have managed to win a World Series MVP Award in the same campaign as winning an LCS MVP. Among this Herculean group are Stargell, Hershiser, Livan Hernandez of the 1997 Florida Marlins and Cole Hamels in 2008.

Over the years, numerous Fall Classic MVPs have also been honored with the Babe Ruth Award, which is given to the player with the best offensive performance in the World Series. The Ruth award, which was awarded for the last time in 2002, was typically handed out several weeks after the Series concluded. It was established by the New York chapter of the Baseball Writers Association of America (BBWAA) and first awarded in 1949, one year after Ruth's death.

A handful of players who dominated for the duration of the postseason have managed to win a World Series MVP Award in the same campaign as winning a LCS Series MVP.

Jackson, 1977

Hershiser, 1988

Gibson, 1964

Robinson, 1966

Koufax, 1963

Eckstein, 2006

CLUBHOUSE CELEBRATIONS

MANY MONTHS BEFORE THE World Series championship is clinched, preparations have already begun for both the on-field celebration and the more raucous revelry that takes place inside the privacy of the clubhouse.

Shortly after a team wins its third game of the World Series — and has an opportunity to clinch the championship at home — MLB officials from departments including special events, PR, broadcasting and sponsorship, as well as the home team's stadium operations group, will meet to discuss the logistical plans for transporting a stage in from beyond the outfield and quickly assembling it behind second base for an on-field awards ceremony following the final out of the clinching game.

SOAKING IT IN Oakland reliever Rollie Fingers gets drenched in champagne after saving the Athletics World Series-clinching 3-2 win over the Reds in 1972.

By presenting the World Series trophy and MVP Award on the field, the Commissioner and MLB's broadcast partners are protected from getting doused by champagne during the wild clubhouse party. But in general, dignitaries realize that being showered in celebratory bubbly is part of the night if they head into the clubhouse.

When the visiting team clinches the Series, the awards are presented inside the clubhouse. The last thing disappointed fans want to see after witnessing their team get eliminated after coming so far is the opposing team hoisting the trophy on their home field. When the home team clinches, though, the on-field ceremony becomes an opportunity for fans to prolong their own stadium jubilation.

BRING ON THE BUBBLY

It starts with finding 60 cases of champagne on short notice. Next comes ordering enough plastic to cover almost all of the clubhouse. Lastly, contracting a cleaning company that can come at any hour.

Although the results may be fun, organizing a clubhouse champagne celebration is far from easy.

"I try to keep guys from spraying three or four bottles at a time and running out," said Jim Schmakel, who manned the Tigers clubhouse during the 1984 and 2006 World Series. "It's a big clubhouse, and I have to make sure everyone has some. It's fun, but I'm working."

For the players, though, the work is definitely over once the corks are popped.

"There are no rules," said Jose Molina who popped the bubbly with the Angels in 2002. "You win, man, and anything goes."

There may not be any real rules to a champagne celebration, but there is a bit of etiquette.

"You try to stay away from guys' eyes," said catcher A.J. Pierzynski. Pierzynski chooses not to wear goggles to protect his eyes from the alcohol like many players do these days. "It's a good burn," he said, "because you're feeling good."

Molina seconded that opinion: "No goggles. With the goggles, you're preparing for it. It's a better feeling when you're taken by surprise."

Sure, a little bit of imbibing goes on during the post-game party, but most of the liquid ends up all over clothing and the carpet. "You just spray and spray everywhere," said pitcher Joba Chamberlain. "Your mouth is open half the time because you're screaming, so you swallow it. But most of the time you're just spraying it."

Added pitcher Scott Linebrink: "I don't think you should walk into a clubhouse during a celebration and expect to keep your dry cleaning in order."

GAME 7: THE GLORY

"Fans are in celebratory mode already and this is a way of sharing in that moment in a personal way," said Brian O'Gara, Major League Baseball's senior director of special events.

Preparations for the victory party begin in the clubhouse around the seventh inning, when clubhouse attendants remove furniture, drape plastic over lockers, and prepare the room for the equivalent of an out-of-control fraternity party. It's a lot of work, which sometimes needs to be undone in a hurry should the game turn. The job can be more challenging if the Series is clinched on the road, since visiting clubhouses tend to be smaller.

By the time the victorious players arrive in the clubhouse, the room is blanketed in vinyl plastic and vibrating with pulsing music. The players quickly break open approximately two dozen cases of beer and 200 bottles of champagne. Most of the alcohol ends up on the floor and dripping from the vinyl. It's a wild scene with players celebrating with family members, team officials, local dignitaries and random celebrities, while a horde of media try to conduct interviews and stay relatively dry.

On nights when a Series-clinching victory is possible, some reporters dress in old clothes and shoes and often even head into the clubhouse wearing ponchos. This is effective for some, but players inevitably seek out journalists they know, especially the local media who have traveled with them all season, and douse them with beer or champagne. A euphoric clubhouse celebration is also a time when a baseball team's hierarchy disappears. It's okay for rookies to soak veterans, for players to soak coaches, the manager, even team executives. Hardly anyone is safe. "Commissioner Selig is the only one we were told we couldn't get. Everyone else is fair game," said catcher A.J. Pierzynski who won the World Series with the White Sox in 2005.

Although most reporters consider it just another occupational hazard, some wait out the initial wave of celebration, heading first to the interview room for press conferences featuring both managers and the MVP of the World Series and then to the somber losers' clubhouse, where the music is turned off and players answer questions in hushed tones, showering and dressing quickly. Back in the winners' clubhouse, the party is still in full swing even by the time the second wave of media arrives, though most of the champagne has been uncorked and the spraying portion of the celebration is mostly over at that point.

It wasn't that long ago when teams celebrated only after a World Series win or and LCS clinch. With the addition of the Division Series in 1995, teams added another beer-soaked party after clinching a Wild Card spot, even though they hadn't won a title of any sort. Although players — and clubhouses — could be worn out by the end of the World Series, the additional merriment has only heightened the intensity of the ultimate victory party. Of course, it likely helps that clubhouse managers ratchet up the champagne order as the postseason progresses — teams usually order 30 cases of bubbly when a playoff spot is clinched, 45 cases for the Division Series win and 60 cases for the LCS and World Series, respectively.

Clubhouse attendants pick up the empty champagne bottles as soon as they're discarded. In recent years, MLB authenticators have been on hand to place holograms on the bottles and log them into the MLB.com database as officially authenticated merchandise. Each player on the winning team receives one of the authenticated bottles to commemorate one of the most memorable celebrations of his life.

LET THE PARTY BEGIN Members of the 2005 Chicago White Sox pass around the World Series Trophy after defeating the Astros, 1-0, to sweep the Series and win the franchise's first world championship in 87 years.

COMMISSIONER'S TROPHY

THE COMMISSIONER'S TROPHY — MORE COMMONLY REFERRED to as "The World Series Trophy" — was first awarded in 1967 when the St. Louis Cardinals defeated the Boston Red Sox. Unlike hockey's Stanley Cup, which is transferred from team to team each season, a new Commissioner's Trophy is created each year and presented to the winning team by the Commissioner of Major League Baseball at the conclusion of the World Series.

The trophy was originally designed by Lawrence Voegele of Owatonna, Minn., and was redesigned slightly in 1999 by Tiffany & Co. Today's edition stands 24 inches tall, excluding the base, measuring 11 inches in diameter. The 30-pound trophy is made of sterling silver and features 30 gold-plated, hand-furled flags — one for each Big League team — which rise above an arched silver baseball with latitude and longitude lines to symbolize the earth. The baseball itself weighs more than 10 pounds and includes the

signature of the commissioner. The previous design included pins at the base of the trophy representing the two teams competing in the Fall Classic. The newer version of the trophy, first presented to the New York Yankees following the 2000 World Series, has an estimated value in materials and labor of $15,000.

The Commissioner's Trophy, unlike the Stanley Cup, Vince Lombardi Trophy (NFL) and Larry O'Brien Trophy (NBA), is the only championship award of the four major U.S. sports not named after an individual person. In 2008, Major League Baseball began showcasing the Commissioner's Trophy prior to the World Series, placing it on display to the public at city halls in Tampa and St. Petersburg, Fla., prior to Game 1, and in Philadelphia before Game 3.

"It's a great way for the fans to get ready and excited before the World Series," said Matt Bourne, MLB's vice president of business public relations.

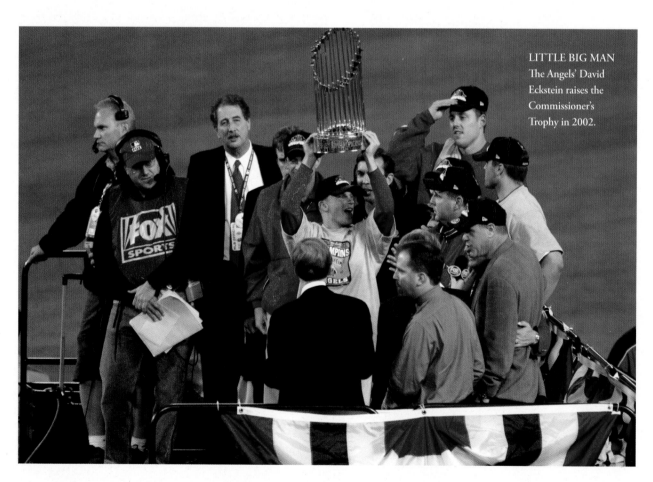

LITTLE BIG MAN The Angels' David Eckstein raises the Commissioner's Trophy in 2002.

PRIZE POSSESSION
The official Major League Baseball World Series trophy, which was awarded to the White Sox in 2005.

WORLD SERIES CHAMPIONS

PARADES

EVERYONE LOVES A PARADE, ESPECIALLY FANS OF THE WORLD SERIES CHAMPIONS. FOR THOSE in charge of planning such celebrations, however, the festivities can present a challenge. In a sport full of superstitious people, nobody wants to jinx a team by preparing for a parade before the victory is sealed. But since the event is usually held the second day after the victory, schedules and routes must be worked out in advance — if ever so quietly.

The victory parade is held soon after the clinching game, but before the excitement dies down and players scatter to their offseason homes. The timeliness of the preparation is especially important for the fans of those teams that clinch the championship on the road.

Joe Torre's Yankees made the ticker-tape trip through New York's Canyon of Heroes into a near-annual event, traversing the lower Manhattan route four times from 1996 to 2000. The route is one mile long and extends through the Financial District along Broadway from Battery Park to City Hall. It has hosted everyone from Nelson Mandela to Pope John Paul II to the 2008 Super Bowl champion New York Giants.

With the celebration parades often snaking around for miles, fans can stake out a good spot or follow the vehicles along. Regardless, it gives the team a chance to have fun and revel in the accomplishment while the city gets a close look at its world champions and cheers them on. Cameramen from MLB Productions even ride on floats with players to capture the experience. In St. Louis in 2006, long-time manager Tony La Russa was chosen to lead the parade in a horse-drawn carriage.

The Chicago White Sox and Florida Marlins enjoyed downtown parades when they took home the trophy, but for teams without central downtown areas, building a parade route can require some creativity.

The Angels, who play in Anaheim, held their parade in 2002 along Main Street in nearby Disneyland and followed it up with a second one that ended with a celebratory rally in the parking lot at their home field, Angels Stadium.

Then there were the Boston Red Sox, who after winning their first World Series in 86 years in 2004, hosted the biggest parade in Major League Baseball history, drawing an estimated 3 million fans along a seven-mile parade route that even included a leg on the Charles River aboard Duck Tour vehicles.

The day before the celebration, Mayor Thomas Menino added the amphibious leg after Boston police expressed concern that the street route would not provide enough space for spectators. The decision proved to be a wise one given the masses that showed up.

Joe Torre's Yankees made the ticker-tape trip through New York's Canyon of Heroes into a near-annual event, traversing the lower Manhattan route four times from 1996 to 2000. The route is one mile long and extends through the Financial District along Broadway from Battery Park to City Hall.

The Phillies' World Series victory in 2008 scuttled initial plans for what would have been the longest parade in World Series history. The Tampa Bay Rays were prepared to travel in a convoy from downtown Tampa over the Gandy Bridge into St. Petersburg and further south to Tropicana Field, a distance of more than 20 miles.

Instead, the Phillies and 45-year-old pitcher Jamie Moyer got to enjoy a parade. Moyer grew up in Sellersville, Pa., and at the age of 17 attended the team's last World Series parade, in 1980.

"Riding in a World Series parade is something you dream about your whole life," Moyer said. "To see how it brings the city together … it's an incredible experience."

CANYON OF HEROES New York celebrates the world champion Yankees in 2000.

LOOKING UP Phillies pitcher Cole Hamels rides down Broad Street in Philadelphia during the team's parade in 2008.

WORLD SERIES SHARES

SINCE THE FIRST MODERN WORLD SERIES WAS CONTESTED in 1903, players on the winning and losing teams have received "shares" of postseason revenues.

The so-called "bonus money" is comprised of 60 percent of gate receipts from the first three games of the Division Series and 60 percent of the gate from the first four games of the League Championship Series and World Series.

World Series shares skyrocketed in 1998 when Fall Classic ticket prices doubled, boosting the players' pool from postseason games to $39.3 million, up from $23.4 million in 1997. Each member of the '98 Yankees voted a full share received about $320,000, significantly more than the '97 Florida Marlins, who received about $190,000 per full share. Shares have been rising incrementally since the early '90s, mirroring the steady increase in revenue generated by the Series.

The money is divided among 12 clubs, the eight that participated in the postseason and the four second-place finishers that were not Wild Card teams, with the World Series champions receiving the largest portions.

WORLD SERIES RINGS

PLAYERS WHO WIN THE WORLD SERIES HAVE TO WAIT MORE than five months for the most tangible reward of their success. That's how long it takes for teams to design and produce the World Series rings. Given the size, detail and materials involved, it's no wonder it takes so long.

The Florida Marlins set a new standard for knuckle-busting jewelry with their 2003 model. With team owner and art dealer Jeffrey Loria overseeing the design, the Marlins' ring weighed in at 70 grams (three and a half ounces) and featured 228 diamonds, 13 rubies and a rare teal diamond for the eye of the Marlin.

"It's huge, a work of art," said Jeff Conine, the only member of the 2003 Marlins who also played on the club's '97 championship team. The following year, Boston was more conservative with their design, which featured a ruby "B" bedecked with 14 large diamonds and another five dozen smaller ones to add sparkle to the ring face.

It was the first Red Sox ring ever issued, as the team's previous titles came before such bands were awarded. The 1922 Giants, who beat the Yankees, became the first team to get rings. At that time, World Series winners typically received watch fobs, medallions or other trinkets. Since 1931, all World Series champs have received rings.

The Red Sox issued a record 500 rings in 2004. Besides players and the coaching staff, much of the World Series-winning front office typically receives rings. Owners also use rings to reward loyal friends and benefactors of the team, and players are offered the chance to purchase additional rings.

Rings are typically presented during a pregame ceremony early the following season. And teams will often hand-deliver rings to players who moved to other clubs during the offseason.

It's believed that rings, designed in recent years by Jostens and InterGold, cost teams between $10,000 and $20,000 apiece depending on the specifics of the design and the size of the order. With rings having become so large, players have been given the opportunity to purchase smaller, less expensive versions for everyday wear. Many players keep their rings in safes, taking them out for special occasions or to serve as motivation.

"I like bling as much as the next guy," said Cliff Floyd, a member of the 1997 championship Marlins. "But you're just not going to wear something like that on a regular basis."

Eric Hinske, who played for the world champion Red Sox in 2007 and the Rays in 2008, was surprised when several of his former teammates showed up in Florida with a personal delivery in April 2008. As Hinske's young teammates passed the ring around, few could have imagined they'd be playing in the Fall Classic six months later.

"They all thought, 'Wouldn't it be awesome to have one of those?'" Hinske said. "It's what you play for, and nobody can ever take it away from you."

BIBLIOGRAPHY

Game 1

Page 26: Curry, Jack. "Former Police Officer Lands Hotel Room for Rays." *The New York Times*. Oct. 28, 2008. p.B16.

Game 2

Page 43: Mellor, David R. *Picture Perfect: Mowing Techniques for Lawns, Landscapes, and Sports*. Chelsea, Mich.; Ann Arbor Press, 2001. p.16.

Game 3

Page 57: Holley, Joe. "Bowie Kuhn; Commissioner Modernized Baseball." *The Washington Post*. March 16, 2007.

Page 58: Footer, Alyson. "Oates steps in to sing anthem for Hall." MLB.com. Oct. 27, 2008.

Page 61: Robbins, Josh. "Flyovers a staple at big sports events, but critics question cost." The *Orlando Sentinel*. Feb. 13, 2008.

Page 64: Bloom, Barry. "Rain Prompts Postponement of Game 4." MLB.com. Oct. 25, 2006.

Page 71: Bellafante, Ginia et al. "The Worst Public Performances of 1996." *Time*. Dec. 23, 1996.

Page 71: Koenig, Bill. "Taking the High-Way." *USA Today Baseball Weekly*. Sept. 17, 1997.

Page 71: Rovell, Darren. "The Business of Blimps." CNBC.com. Sept. 3, 2008.

Game 4

Page 92: Bialik, Carl. "Using Stats to Try and Take Roger Federer's Measure." The *Wall Street Journal*. Sept. 12, 2005.

Game 5

Page 108: Kepner, Tyler. "A Dream Call for Harry Kalas, Vocie of the Phillies." *The New York Times*. Oct. 27, 2008.

Game 6

Page 116: Gelles, Jeff. "Counterfeit Phillies Gear a Big Business." The *Philadelphia Inquirer*. Oct. 28, 2008.

Page 122: Dodd, Mike. "MLB Authenticators Give Seal of Approval to Genuine Articles." *USA Today*. July 16, 2008.

Page 125: Rovell, Darren. "The Cork that Never Popped." CNBC.com. Oct. 15, 2008.

Page 125: Sandomir, Richard. "Munson Memorabilia Fetches High Prices." *The New York Times*. July 14, 2008.

Page 125: Williams, Pete. "Real McCoy?" *USA Today Baseball Weekly*. Aug. 12, 1992.

Game 7

Page 139: Lemire, Joe. "Phillies' World Series Merchandise Still a Hot Commodity." SI.com, Nov. 19, 2008.

Page 151: Fallstrom, R.B. "St. Louis Honors Cards with Victory Parade." The Associated Press. October 29, 2006.

Page 151: Slack, Donovan and Andrew Ryan. "Red Sox Rolling Rally will be Similar to 2004." The *Boston Globe*. Oct. 29, 2007.

Page 154: Edes, Gordon. "Jewelry in Store: Sox' Return Home Has a Nice Ring to It." The *Boston Globe*. April 8, 2008.

CREDITS

BRAD MANGIN/MLB PHOTOS: COVER, 49, 59, 147, 148

MILES KENNEDY/MLB PHOTOS: 2-3, 152-153

RON VESELY/MLB PHOTOS: 5, 84-85, 94, 102-103, 149

BETTMANN/CORBIS: 6, 18, 52, 107, 144

RICH PILLING/MLB PHOTOS: 8, 14, 16-17, 20-21, 23, 40-41, 60, 66-67, 69, 91, 98, 123, 131, 132, 135, 142, 150

FPG/GETTY IMAGES: 10, 32, 53, 140

COURTESY OF MLB: 12, 13

MLB PHOTOS/GETTY IMAGES: 24

NBLA/MLB PHOTOS: 25, 109, 126, 128-129Z

BILL SAURO/THE NEW YORK TIMES/GETTY IMAGES: 27

JED JACOBSOHN/GETTY IMAGES: 30

STEPHEN GREEN/MLB PHOTOS: 37, 47, 104-105

AP PHOTO: 38-39, 145

JERRY WACHTER/MLB PHOTOS: 42

EZRA SHAW/GETTY IMAGES: 43

PAUL CUNNINGHAM/MLB PHOTOS: 44-45, 50, 70, 86, 120-121

STEPHEN DUNN/GETTY IMAGES: 54-55, 62-63

TONY DEJAK/AP PHOTO: 56

BRIAN BAHR/GETTY IMAGES: 61

ELISE AMENDOLA/AP PHOTO: 65, 144

BOB ROWAN; PROGRESSIVE IMAGE/ CORBIS: 72-73

TAMPA BAY RAYS/MLB PHOTOS: 74

OLEN COLLECTION/DIAMOND IMAGES/GETTY IMAGES: 76

DAVID KOHL: 79

GEORGE SILK/TIME LIFE PICTURES/ GETTY IMAGES: 81

RHONA WISE/EPA/CORBIS: 82-83

MARK CUNNINGHAM/MLB PHOTOS: 89

RONALD MARTINEZ/GETTY IMAGES: 93

MICHAEL ZAGARIS/MLB PHOTOS: 96

DAVID LILIENSTEIN/MLB PHOTOS: 101

TIM PARKER/MLB PHOTOS: 111

MARY SCHWALM/AP PHOTO/TACO BELL: 112

DOUG PENSINGER/GETTY IMAGES: 114

JIM ROGASH/GETTY IMAGES: 116

MARK KAUFFMAN//TIME LIFE PICTURES/GETTY IMAGES: 119

KIDWILER COLLECTION/DIAMOND IMAGES/GETTY IMAGES: 124

TIM ROSKE/AP PHOTO: 130

CHARLES KRUPA/AP PHOTO: 133

JOHN REID III/MLB PHOTOS: 136

POOL/GETTY IMAGES: 138, 140

JIM MCISAAC/GETTY IMAGES: 139

LENNY IGNELZI/AP PHOTO: 141

WALTER IOOSS JR./SPORTS ILLUSTRATED/GETTY IMAGES: 143, 144

LOUIS REQUENA/MLB PHOTOS: 144

HERB SCHARFMAN/SPORTS IMAGERY/GETTY IMAGES: 144

LENNOX MCLENDON/AP PHOTO: 144

INDEX